Edited by Eric Kroll, Introduction by Ron Shelton, Captions by Gabriel Schechter

# NEIL LEIFER

## BALLET IN THE DIRT: THE GOLDEN AGE OF BASEBALL

**TASCHEN**

HONG KONG  KÖLN  LONDON  LOS ANGELES  MADRID  PARIS  TOKYO

*For my brother, Howie*

Take me out to the ball game,

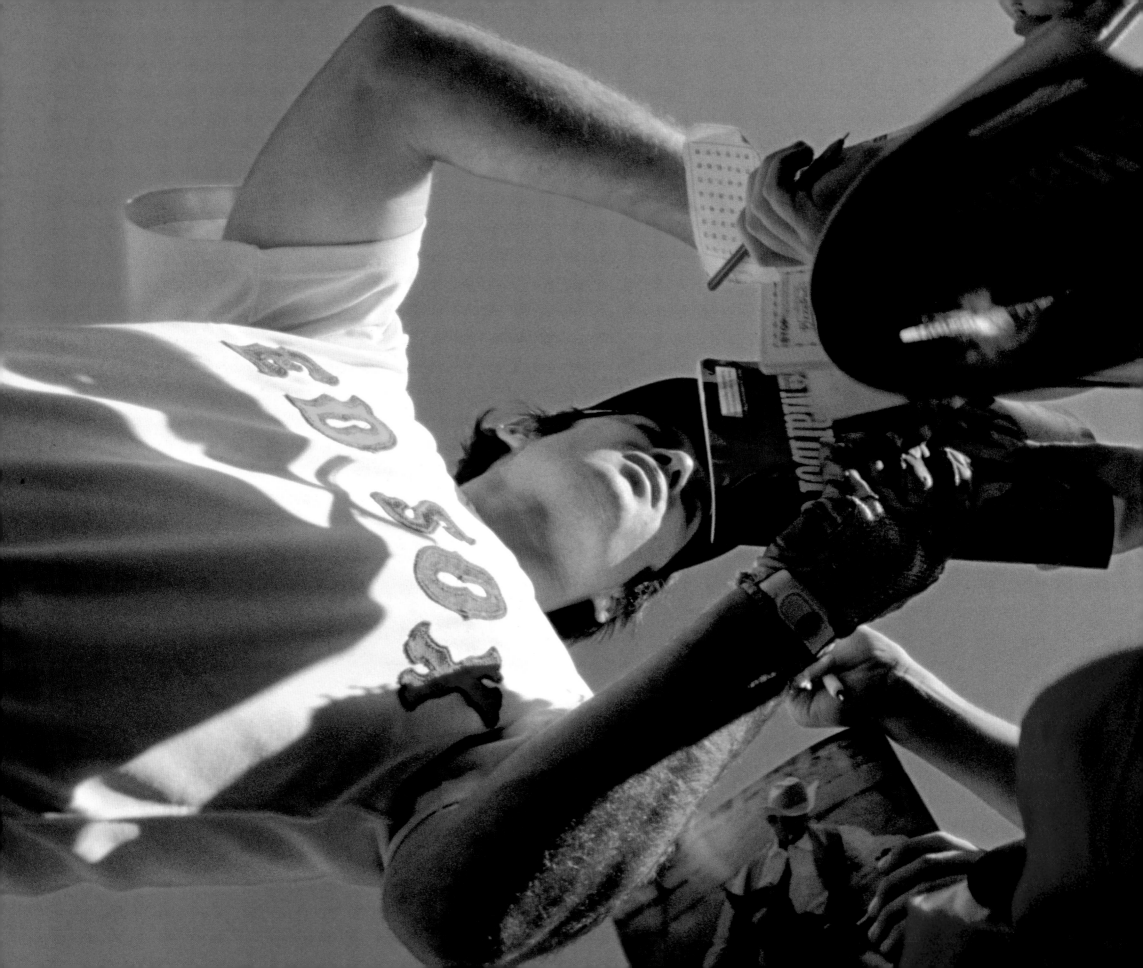

Take me out to the crowd.

I don't care if
I never get back.

Let me root, root, root
for the home team,

If they don't win it's a shame.

For it's one, two,
   three strikes, you're out,

*At the old ball game.*

# NEIL LEIFER, CASEY STENGEL, VIDA BLUE AND AN EARLY WYNN*
## —Preface by Eric Kroll

A great novelist puts the reader inside the minds and bodies of his fictional characters. That's how Neil Leifer takes photographs of professional baseball. I spent hours sitting next to Howie, Neil's brother, with a magnifying loupe, combing through Neil Leifer's black and white contact sheets and sheets of 35mm color slides. Somehow he had every angle of every minute of every game (of significance) for two wonderful decades. How did he do it?

When a professional baseball player gets to the major leagues it is called getting to "the Show." Neil shot the Show. Behind the curtain, in the balcony, dressing room, orchestra … even in the orchestra pit, better known as the dugout. He was everywhere, seemingly at the same time.

He was the only photographer at field level when Juan Marichal, Giants pitcher and batter, smashed Dodgers catcher John Roseboro in the head with a baseball bat. He caught Hank Aaron rounding the bases after hitting his 715th home run (beating Babe Ruth's record) and being congratulated by the Dodgers' short stop and second baseman, opponents … unheard of in baseball history on all levels, and Neil got it on film.

One has to remember that the beginning of Neil's life was also the beginning of his career as a professional photographer. He grew up in the field … literally. A cherub with panache and a long lens. And you can see his bravado and his complete and utter pleasure of being where he was, in the photo of him sitting next to Stan Musial in the St. Louis dugout.

To me, there is a distinct difference between how he shot as a freelancer and how he shot on assignment for *Sports Illustrated*. Again this distinction parallels his maturity as a photographer. I particularly love the early Leifer photographs, but maybe that's because they are of the oldest ball players. He caught the Duke, Musial, and Casey Stengel as they were closing the door on Hall of Fame careers. But he more than made up for it with time spent photographing the likes of Roberto Clemente at the apex of his career. He was Clemente's shadow in the team hotel after a game, in the trainer's room easing sore muscles, playing right field, as he rounded the bases, and as he was hitting.

Neil would disagree with me. He feels there was no difference in his work from when he was a freelancer and on assignment. He feels his approach was the same. Two things changed when he went to work for *Sports Illustrated*: He got better equipment and he got credentials.

No one expected Clemente's career to be foreshortened, but that's the way Leifer shot it. That's the way he covered any baseball player. Memorable. The definitive portrait in action and in repose —Frank Robinson, Brooks Robinson, Roger Maris, and on and on.

Leifer's crowd shots blanket the sphere of human emotion. Shock, joy, elation, disappointment. And it is art. I'm a photographer. I understand composition and I saw it in his photographs time and time again on the field, but I saw it equally in Leifer's photographs of the people in stands.

Neil was emphatic that his photographs chosen for this book be in focus.

Personally, I would sacrifice sharpness for mood. Not Neil. I went through thousands and thousands of contact sheets and color slides, and Neil and his brother Howie knew every image … by heart. When looking at the dummy for this book Neil would say (occasionally), "I've got a better picture than that one," and he did.

When Leifer began taking baseball photographs, newspaper photographers stayed in the mezzanine press box. Neil went to field level. In sports photography it is "follow focus." To be a good sports photographer one had to have superior hand-eye co-ordination. The standard baseball lenses were the 300, 400, and 600mm. Neil's left hand was constantly on the focus ring and his right hand, his trigger finger, was on shutter release, shooting in sequence. Neil shot with two cameras, sometimes three, each coupled to a heavy motor drive, with the three long lenses, or the 2000mm. He also used a 180, 105, 80, 50, 35 and, for inside the clubhouse, a 24mm lens. Plus his Widelux (140-degree panoramic) camera for the stadium shots.

When he first started taking photographs of baseball he shot with black and white Tri-X film and Ektachrome and, when the light permitted, Kodachrome ASA 10, a very slow film to capture action with! Later there was Kodachrome 64 and finally Kodachrome 100. There is very little latitude when shooting color slide film and Kodachrome can't be "pushed" (exposure compensation done in the development) … at least it couldn't back then.

Difficult lighting conditions from deep shadow to bright sunlight … slow film … pressure to get the definitive photograph at the decisive moment for the showcase publication, *Sports Illustrated* — Neil Leifer did it day after day, year after year, and blanketed professional baseball with great photographs. This book is that blanket spread out across the golden age of baseball.

Neil was on second base by the time I got to first. What I mean is, his eye and his life experience exceeds me by four years. Fortunately, he recorded magnificently (cleanly, honestly) the cornerstone of my youthful memories.

A teenage Neil delivered sandwiches for the Stage Delicatessen on 7th Avenue and 54th Street to, among others, many of the Yankees living nearby in apartments rented for the season and to the Life magazine photo studio around the corner. Seeing early photographs of a very youthful, defiant, freckle-faced Neil Leifer toting cameras … it must have helped to have known one of his subjects and his new co-workers from a different lifetime. I mean, he looks like a child with a long lens … not yet a seasoned professional, which he became.

I suspect he has always been in front of the curve … ahead of the game. Maybe that chutzpah came from growing up in the real Lower East Side of lower Manhattan. Certainly he found himself, not at the library, sometimes in the darkroom, but often behind home plate … or out in left field. I once asked him if he ever felt lonely out there in the center field bleachers with a long lens and a couple of hot dogs. He looked at me like I was crazy and said, with his eyes

lighting up as they often do, "No, it was exciting! I couldn't believe someone was paying me to go to a ballgame!"

It was ballet in the dirt, cheered by a crowd huddled in a cavernous place, lit by a fading late afternoon sun. And in the crowd I can just make out a very serious young man intently surveying the baseball diamond, making it his own.

"The really great sports photographers — when they get lucky — they don't miss."
—Neil Leifer

* *Neil Leifer takes (these) photographs and makes films. Casey Stengel managed the New York Yankees to 10 pennants and seven World Series, five in a row. Vida Blue pitched for the Oakland A's and later the San Francisco Giants. He won the Cy Young Award in 1971. Early Wynn played for the Washington Senators, the Cleveland Indians, and the Chicago White Sox. Five times he won 20 games or more in a season, and he played in seven All-Star games, plus won a Cy Young Award in 1959.*

### The Polo Grounds, April 21, 1963

**OPPOSITE** Bleacher fans view Coogan's Bluff perched above the sweeping grandstands of the Polo Grounds. Formerly home to the New York Giants, the venerable ballpark began its final season in 1963 hosting the hapless Mets.

**GEGENÜBER** Von den Bleachers blicken die Fans auf Coogan's Bluff oberhalb der weiten Haupttribüne der Polo

Grounds. Das ehrwürdige Stadion, einst Heimat der New York Giants, erlebte 1963 seine letzte Saison - als Spielstätte der glücklosen Mets.

**PAGE CI-CONTRE** Vue sur le Coogan's Bluff (promontoire rocheux situé dans l'Upper Manhattan) qui s'élève au-dessus des tribunes circulaires du Polo Grounds. Le vénérable stade a d'abord abrité les New York Giants.

### The '58 Series, New York Yankees vs. Milwaukee Braves, World Series game 5, Yankee Stadium, October 6, 1958

**PAGE 26** Neil, still wet behind the ears at age 16, shot a young Hank Aaron at bat in the '58 World Series. Many innings later, he shot him again as a seasoned veteran the night he broke Babe Ruth's hallowed home run record.

**SEITE 26** 1958 fotografierte Neil, mit 16 noch nicht trocken hinter den Ohren, in der World Series einen jungen Hank Aaron beim Schlag. Viele Innings später fotografierte er ihn wieder – als erfahrenen Veteranen,

der an jenem Abend gerade den geheiligten Homerun-Rekord von Babe Ruth gebrochen hatte.

**PAGE 26** Neil, seize ans et encore inexpérimenté, photographie un jeune Hank Aaron à la batte lors des World Series de 1958. De nombreuses saisons plus tard, il photographiera encore le vétéran aguerri le soir où il battra le vénérable record de coups de circuit de Babe Ruth.

# NEIL LEIFER, CASEY STENGEL, VIDA BLUE UND EIN EARLY WYNN*

## —Vorwort von Eric Kroll

Genauso, wie man sich bei einem guten Romanautor in die Gedanken und Handlungen seiner Charaktere versetzt, ergeht es einem, wenn man sich Neil Leifers Fotos von Baseballprofis anschaut. Ich habe stundenlang mit einer Lupe neben Neils Bruder Howie gesessen und Kontaktstreifen von Schwarz-Weiß-Fotos sowie Bögen von 35-Millimeter-Farbdias durchkämmt. Irgendwie hat Neil über einen Zeitraum von zwei Jahrzehnten von jedem Spiel jeden Blickwinkel und jede Minute erfasst. Wie hat er das nur gemacht?

Wenn ein Baseballprofi in die oberen Ligen aufsteigt, dann wird er Teil der „Show". Neil hat die Show fotografiert. Hinter dem Vorhang, auf der Galerie, in der Umkleidekabine, im Orchester … ja, sogar im Orchestergraben, den man gemeinhin *dugout* nennt. Er war überall und scheinbar auch überall zur selben Zeit.

Er war der einzige Fotograf am Spielfeldrand, als Juan Marichal, Pitcher und Schlagmann der Giants, dem Fänger der Dodgers, John Roseboro, das Schlagholz auf den Kopf knallte.

Er war da, als Hank Aaron bei seinem 715. Homerun (mit dem er den Rekord von Babe Ruth brach) von Base zu Base lief und als der Shortstop und der zweite Baseman der gegnerischen Dodgers ihm gratulierten. So etwas hatte es in der Geschichte des Baseball noch nie gegeben, in keiner Spielklasse. Neil hat es auf Film.

Man muss daran erinnern, dass Neils Leben zu dem Zeitpunkt so richtig anfing, als auch seine Karriere als Berufsfotograf begann. Er wuchs im wahrsten Sinne des Wortes auf dem Spielfeld auf. Ein Cherub mit Elan und Teleobjektiven. Was für ein Draufgänger er war und wie er es durch und durch genoss, da zu sein, wo er war, sieht man auf dem Foto, das ihn neben Stan Musial im *dugout* der St. Louis Cardinals zeigt.

Für mich gibt es einen deutlichen Unterschied zwischen seinen Aufnahmen als Freelancer und denen, die er im Auftrag von *Sports Illustrated* schoss. Hier sieht man, wie er auch als Fotograf erwachsen wurde. Als er Duke Snider, Stan Musial und Casey Stengel fotografierte, gingen deren Karrieren, die sie in die Hall of Fame führten, bereits langsam zu Ende. Aber er machte das mehr als wett mit der Zeit, die er dem Fotografieren von Spielern wie Roberto Clemente auf dem Höhepunkt von dessen Karriere widmete. Leifer verfolgte ihn wie ein Schatten, so wie ein Verteidiger den gegnerischen Außenstürmer verfolgt – nach einem Spiel im Mannschaftshotel, in der Kabine des Trainers beim Lockern der Muskeln, wenn er im *right field* spielte, wenn er von einem Base zum nächsten lief und wenn er schlug.

Neil würde mir nicht zustimmen. Er sieht keinen Unterschied in seiner Arbeit als Freelancer und als Fotograf im Auftrag von *Sports Illustrated*. Er meint, sein Ansatz sei immer derselbe gewesen. Zwei Dinge jedenfalls änderten sich, als er begann, für *Sports Illustrated* zu arbeiten. Er bekam eine bessere Ausrüstung, und er bekam die nötigen Akkreditierungen.

Niemand konnte damit rechnen, dass Clementes Karriere so tragisch und so früh zu Ende gehen würde, aber Leifer schien beim Fotografieren auf alles vorbereitet. Er fotografierte jeden Baseballspieler so. Unvergesslich, für die Nachwelt. Das definitive Porträt – in Action ebenso wie in einer Ruhepause: Frank Robinson, Brooks Robinson, Roger Maris und so weiter und so fort.

Auf Leifers Fotos von Zuschauern sieht man das ganze Spektrum menschlicher Gefühle: Schock, Freude, Begeisterung, Enttäuschung. Und das ist Kunst. Ich bin selbst Fotograf. Ich weiß, was Bildaufbau bedeutet, und ich habe diese Komposition wieder und wieder auf seinen Fotos auf dem Platz erkannt, aber ebenso in seinen Bildern der Menschen auf den Tribünen.

Neil bestand darauf, dass für dieses Buch nur gestochen scharfe Fotos ausgewählt würden. Ich persönlich hätte die Schärfe gern zugunsten der Stimmung geopfert. Nicht so Neil. Ich arbeitete mich durch Tausende und Abertausende von Kontaktstreifen und Diapositiven, und Neil und Bruder Howie kannten jedes einzelne Bild – auswendig. Als wir uns den Dummy dieses Buches ansahen, meinte Neil (gelegentlich): „Davon habe ich ein besseres Bild." Und es stimmte.

Als Leifer anfing, beim Baseball zu fotografieren, arbeiteten die Zeitungsfotografen aus einem Pressestand im ersten Rang. Neil ging runter, auf die Spielfeldebene. Bei einem guten Sportfotografen müssen Hand und Auge hervorragend koordiniert sein. Die Standardobjektive beim Baseball hatten Brennweiten von 300, 400 und 600 Millimetern. Neils linke Hand war ununterbrochen am Schärfering tätig, während er rechts immer wieder auf den Auslöser drückte und so ganze Bildfolgen schoss. Er arbeitete mit zwei, manchmal auch drei Kameras, jede verbunden mit einem schweren Motor für den Filmaufzug, und setzte die drei Teleobjektive oder ein 2000-Millimeter-Objektiv ein. Außerdem benutzte er Objektive mit Brennweiten von 180, 105, 80, 50, 35 und – im Klubhaus – 24 Millimetern. Dazu im Stadion seine Widelux-Kamera für 140-Grad-Panoramaaufnahmen.

Anfangs benutzte er beim Baseball Tri-X-Schwarz-Weiß- sowie Ektachrome-Farbfilme und, wenn es das Licht erlaubte, auch Kodachrome ASA 10, einen sehr langsamen Film, und das zur Aufnahme von Sportszenen! Später nahm er dann Kodachrome 64 und schließlich Kodachrome 100. Die Filme für Farb-Diapositive lassen bei der Belichtung nur einen sehr geringen Ermessensspielraum, und den Kodachrome kann man auch nicht schneller machen … Jedenfalls konnte man es damals nicht.

Schwierige Lichtverhältnisse von tiefstem Schatten bis zu gleißendem Sonnenschein … langsamer Film … der Druck, im richtigen Augenblick *das* Foto für *Sports Illustrated* zu schießen … Neil schaffte es Tag für Tag, Jahr für Jahr und schuf mit seinen Fotos ein überwältigendes Porträt des Profibaseball. Dieses Buch ist das Porträt des goldenen Baseballzeitalters.

Neil hatte schon das zweite Base erreicht, als ich beim ersten ankam. Ich will damit sagen, dass er mir, was das Auge und die Lebenserfahrung angeht, vier Jahre voraus ist. Glücklicherweise hat er den Grundpfeiler meiner jugendlichen Erinnerungen wunderbar (sauber, ehrlich) festgehalten.

Der Teenager Neil lieferte Sandwiches für „Stage Delicatessen" Ecke 7th Avenue und 54th Street aus – unter anderem an viele Spieler der Yankees, die in der Nähe für die Dauer der Spielzeit Wohnungen gemietet hatten, und an das Fotostudio der Illustrierten *Life* gleich um die Ecke. Man sieht Fotos, auf denen ein sehr jugendlicher, kecker und sommersprossiger Neil Leifer Kameras schleppt, und denkt sich, dass es doch von Vorteil gewesen sein muss, einige seiner Hauptdarsteller und seiner neuen Kollegen aus einem früheren Leben zu kennen. Ich meine, er sieht aus wie ein Kind mit einem Teleobjektiv … nicht wie der erfahrene Profi aus späteren Tagen.

Ich vermute, er ist immer schon aus der Kurve raus gewesen, dem Spiel immer einen Schritt voraus. Vielleicht rührte diese Chuzpe daher, dass er an der *wahren* Lower East Side von Manhattan aufgewachsen war. Ohne Frage hielt er sich selten in der Bibliothek, häufiger in der Dunkelkammer und am meisten hinter dem Schlagmal oder draußen im *left field*. Ich hab ihn mal gefragt, ob er sich nicht gelangweilt habe auf den Zuschauersitzen in Höhe des *center field*, allein mit einem Teleobjektiv und ein paar Hotdogs. Er sah mich an, als wäre ich verrückt geworden, und sagte, während seine Augen aufblitzten wie so oft: „Nein, es war aufregend! Ich konnte einfach nicht glauben, dass mich jemand dafür bezahlte, zu einem Baseballspiel zu gehen."

Es war ein Ballett im Staub, bejubelt von einer Menschenmenge, dicht zusammengedrängt in einer riesigen Höhle, dem Stadion, beleuchtet von der langsam verblassenden Nachmittagssonne. Und in der Menge kann ich nur einen einzelnen sehr ernsthaften jungen Mann ausmachen, der gespannt das Baseballspielfeld betrachtet und es in sich aufnimmt.

„Die wirklich bedeutenden Sportfotografen bekommen jedes Bild – wenn sie Glück haben."
– Neil Leifer

* Neil Leifer macht Fotos (die in diesem Buch) und dreht Filme. Casey Stengel führte die New York Yankees zu zehn Liga-Meisterschaften und sieben World Series, davon fünf in Folge. Vida Blue war Pitcher der Oakland A's und später der San Francisco Giants. 1971 gewann er den Cy Young Award als bester Pitcher. Early Wynn spielte für die Washington Senators, die Cleveland Indians und die Chicago White Sox. Fünfmal gewann er 20 oder mehr Spiele innerhalb einer Saison, siebenmal stand er in einer All-Star-Mannschaft und gewann außerdem 1959 einen Cy Young Award.

# NEIL LEIFER, CASEY STENGEL, VIDA BLUE ET EARLY WYNN*
## —Préface Eric Kroll

Un grand romancier installe son lecteur dans l'esprit et dans le corps de ses personnages de fiction. Neil Leifer procédait de la même façon lorsqu'il photographiait le baseball professionnel. Une loupe grossissante à la main, j'ai passé des heures à côté de Howie, le frère de Neil, afin d'explorer les planches contact en noir et blanc et les planches diapositives couleur 35mm. C'est incroyable, mais il a toujours su saisir chaque aspect de chaque minute de chaque rencontre (importante) et ceci pendant deux décennies stupéfiantes. Comment y est-il parvenu ?

Lorsqu'un joueur de baseball professionnel arrive en ligue majeure, on dit de lui qu'il entre dans le « Show ». Neil photographiait le Show. Derrière le rideau, au balcon, dans les loges, à l'orchestre... même si la fosse est mieux connue sous le nom d'abri des joueurs. Il était partout, comme doué du don d'ubiquité.

Il est le seul photographe présent lorsque Juan Marichal, lanceur et batteur des Giants, assène un coup de batte sur la tête de John Roseboro, le receveur des Dodgers.

Il photographie Hank Aaron qui fait le tour des bases après avoir frappé son sept-cent-quinzième coup de circuit, battant ainsi le record de Babe Ruth. Le bloqueur et le joueur de deuxième base des Dodgers le félicitent. Ses adversaires également, ce qui est inédit dans toute l'histoire du baseball. Neil a saisi ces moments sur pellicule.

N'oublions pas que le début de la vie de Neil correspond au début de sa carrière de photographe professionnel. Il a grandi sur le terrain... littéralement. Un petit ange plein de panache avec son téléobjectif. On lit sa fierté, une joie entière et non dissimulée, sur la photo où on le voit aux côtés de Stan Musial dans l'abri des joueurs de Saint-Louis.

Selon moi, il y a une différence évidente entre les images prises en tant que freelance et celles commandées par *Sports Illustrated*. Cette distinction reflète sa maturation en tant qu'artiste. J'adore plus particulièrement les photos de jeunesse de Leifer. Peut-être parce qu'il y couche les joueurs les plus anciens. Il n'a pu immortaliser Duke, Musial ou Casey Stengel as qu'au moment où les portes du Temple de la renommée se refermaient derrière eux. Ce qu'il a compensé en photographiant si souvent Roberto Clemente, entre autres, au sommet de sa carrière. Il était l'ombre de Clemente dans son hôtel après une rencontre, dans la salle d'exercices quand il décontractait ses muscles endoloris, ou lorsqu'il jouait champ droit, qu'il faisait le tour des bases, qu'il frappait.

Neil ne serait pas d'accord avec moi. Il pense qu'il n'y a aucune différence entre son travail indépendant et ses commandes. Pour lui, son approche est restée la même et, lorsqu'il a été engagé par *Sports Illustrated*, il a seulement obtenu un meilleur équipement et des accréditations. Personne ne s'attendait à ce que la carrière de Clemente fût si courte, mais c'est ainsi que Leifer l'a photographiée. C'est ainsi qu'il photographiait tous les joueurs de baseball. C'est inoubliable. Le portrait ultime à la fois dans l'action et au repos : Frank Robinson, Brooks Robinson, Roger Maris, parmi tant d'autres.

Les foules de Leifer embrassent toute la sphère des émotions humaines.

Choc, joie, exultation, déception. Et c'est de l'art. Je suis moi-même photographe, je comprends les difficultés de la composition et, pourtant, elles paraissent abolies dans ses photos du terrain ou des tribunes.

Neil a insisté très énergiquement : les œuvres choisies pour ce livre devaient être parfaitement nettes. Personnellement, j'aurais sacrifié la précision à l'atmosphère. Mais pas Neil. J'ai exploré des milliers de planches contact et de diapositives couleur... Neil et son frère Howie les connaissaient toutes par cœur. Lorsque nous regardions la maquette de cet ouvrage, Neil affirmait parfois : « J'ai une meilleure photo. » Et c'était le cas.

Quand Leifer a commencé à immortaliser le monde du baseball, les photographes de presse s'entassaient dans la tribune qui leur était réservée. Neil, lui, est descendu au niveau du terrain. Dans la photographie sportive, on met au point en permanence. Et donc, on se doit d'avoir une excellente coordination entre l'œil et la main. Pour le baseball, on utilise traditionnellement des objectifs de 300, 400 et 600mm. La main gauche de Neil virevoltait sur la bague tandis que son index droit, posé sur le déclencheur, mitraillait la scène. Neil avait toujours deux ou trois boîtiers, dotés d'un moteur puissant, couplés à ces trois téléobjectifs ou à un super-téléobjectif de 2000mm. Il gardait à portée de main un 180mm, un 105mm, un 80mm, un 50mm, un 35mm et, pour les prises de vue à l'intérieur du club-house, un 24mm. Ainsi que son appareil Widelux (panoramique couvrant 140 degrés) pour les photos d'ensemble.

Lorsqu'il s'est mis au baseball, il photographiait en noir et blanc : films Tri-X et Ektachrome et, quand la lumière le permettait, Kodachrome 10 ASA (extrêmement lent pour une action !) Plus tard, il est passé au Kodachrome 64 et enfin au 100. On a très peu de marge avec des diapositives couleur et les Kodachrome ne peuvent être poussés (on compensait l'exposition au cours du développement)... enfin, ne pouvaient pas à l'époque.

Conditions de lumière difficiles (de l'ombre la plus profonde jusqu'au plein soleil)... des films lents... la pression pour obtenir la photo ultime du moment décisif pour une publication prestigieuse : *Sports Illustrated*. Neil Leifer l'a fait jour après jour, année après année et a couvert tout le baseball professionnel de ses photographies géniales. Cet ouvrage embrasse à son tour cet âge d'or du baseball.

J'arrivais à peine sur la première base que Neil touchait la deuxième. En fait, il a toujours eu quatre ans d'avance sur moi quant au regard et à l'expérience. Par chance, il a enregistré magnifiquement (avec précision et honnêteté) la pierre angulaire de mes souvenirs de jeunesse.

Adolescent, Neil travaillait au Stage Delicatessen à l'angle de la 7ème avenue et de la 54ème rue. Il livrait des sandwichs à de nombreux membres des Yankees (entre autres) qui vivaient dans des appartements loués pour la saison, mais aussi au studio du magazine photographique *Life*, situé dans le quartier. En voyant les photographies de Neil jeune, l'air impertinent et le visage constellé de taches de rousseur, les boîtiers qui brinquebalent autour du cou... connaître

certains de ses sujets et ses confrères plus âgés ne l'a sans doute pas desservi. Franchement, on dirait un gosse avec un objectif trop grand pour lui... et pas le professionnel aguerri qu'il est devenu par la suite.

Je le soupçonne d'avoir toujours été en avance, d'avoir toujours su garder l'initiative. Cette *chutzpah*, cette véritable impudence, provient peut-être du fait qu'il a grandi dans le *vrai* Lower East Side de Manhattan. Évidemment, on ne le trouvait guère à la bibliothèque. Parfois dans la chambre noire, mais plus souvent derrière le marbre ou dans le champ gauche. Un jour, je lui ai demandé s'il ne s'était jamais senti seul dans les gradins devant le champ centre avec son téléobjectif et ses deux hot-dogs. Il m'a regardé comme si j'étais fou. Son regard s'est illuminé – comme souvent chez lui – et il m'a affirmé : « Bien sûr que non, j'étais tellement excité ! Je n'arrivais pas à croire qu'on me payait pour voir un match ! »

Un ballet dans la poussière, acclamé par une foule blottie dans un stade immense, éclairé par le pâle soleil d'une fin d'après-midi. Et dans le public, je distingue un jeune homme à l'air très sérieux qui surveille attentivement le terrain, qui le fait sien.

« Quand les grands photographes sportifs ont une chance... ils ne la ratent pas. »
— Neil Leifer

*\*Neil Leifer est photographe et réalisateur. Casey Stengel a conduit les New York Yankees vers dix titres et sept World Series (Rencontres organisées entre les équipes championnes des deux ligues (« américaine » et « nationale ») de la ligue majeure (Major League Baseball)), dont cinq d'affilée ; Vida Blue a lancé pour les Oakland A's, puis pour les San Francisco Giants. Il a gagné le Cy Young Award (Trophée annuel remis au meilleur lanceur de chaque ligue) en 1971. Early Wynn a joué pour les Washington Senators, les Cleveland Indians et les Chicago White Sox. Il a remporté cinq fois plus de vingt rencontres dans la saison et a participé à sept All-Star games (Rencontre annuelle disputée entre deux équipes représentant chacune une ligue et composées de joueurs élus par le public). Il a en outre décroché le Cy Young Award en 1959.*

### Brooklyn Dodgers, Ebbets Field

**OPPOSITE** Ebbets Field, home of the Brooklyn Dodgers from 1913 to 1957, featured baseball's most eccentric right field. A right fielder never knew which way the ball would bounce if it got past him.

**GEGENÜBER** Ebbets Field, von 1913 bis 1957 die Heimat der Brooklyn Dodgers, wies die ausgefallenste rechte Spielfeldseite auf. Ein Spieler auf diesem Teil des Platzes nie wusste, wohin ein Ball springen würde, wenn er an ihm vorbeiflog ...

**PAGE CI-CONTRE** Ebbets Field a accueilli les Brooklyn Dodgers de 1913 à 1957. On y trouvait un champ droit des plus curieux. Le joueur de champ droit de savoir de quel côté la balle allait rebondir si elle lui passait par-dessus.

# IT WAS GOLDEN: BASEBALL IN THE '60s AND '70s

*—Introduction by Ron Shelton*

When Martin Luther King was writing his letters from the Birmingham jail, when JFK and then his brother were gunned down, when body counts and flag-draped coffins were part of our TV news diet, when Jimi and Janis, free love, Kent State, and civil rights marches to Selma, Alabama, were our daily bread, there existed a parallel universe mostly untouched by these events. There existed the golden age of baseball.

**Like most golden ages, I suppose, we didn't know we were in one 'til it was over.** I know. I made my living at this game as "property" of the Baltimore Orioles. The Vietnam War was never discussed on team bus trips or in hotels in Little Rock, Amarillo, or Louisville — it was as if the war didn't exist. In fact, baseball players were consumed with only two things, then as now.

First, their own statistics, because that is how they are judged. Every hitter knows that when you're suffering through a "one for six" batting slump, your next at-bat is the difference between hitting .143 or .286. Two for seven is .286—you know that as soon as the ball gets through the infield and you're running to first base.

The second thing baseball players were consumed by was getting laid. Guys chased women. Women chased guys. And most of the time there wasn't much chasing required. Stats and chicks, numbers and women, bar to bar, ballpark to ballpark—it was an endless journey to hit, to score, to throw the heat, to make the play, to score the ladies—ongoing and forever. Amen. The church of baseball had no assassinations, no Vietnam, and no protest marches. There was only the game.

Through Neil Leifer's eyes we see the beauty of baseball in the 1960s and '70s—the best the game has ever been. The gods are everywhere in Leifer's photographs: Mantle, Mays, Clemente, Koufax … And they look like us, only better. These aren't men with artificially built bodies. These often aren't even very big men—Henry Aaron was slight, Willie Mays was short, and Denny McLain? He's the chunky guy playing a B3 organ in the Holiday Inn lounge. He's also the last pitcher to win 30 games.

The game was different then. It was better. That's not nostalgia, that's a fact, and, as Casey Stengel said, "You could look it up"—but if you did look it up you'd discover that Casey stole the line from James Thurber, American humorist. After all, it's OK to steal in baseball.

Heroes were everywhere—we had McCovey, Mathews, and Maury Wills. Even the immortals like Ted Williams and Stan Musial played into the '60s. And the Robinsons, Frank and Brooks, on one team—the Baltimore Orioles, no less. The same team had four 20-game winners in '71. Listen to the names from the era—Gibby, Reggie, Pops, Maz and Yaz and Yogi. First names were enough. Thurman Munson, a Midwesterner, played for the New York Yankees and Bill "Spaceman" Lee, a Southern California socialist, played for the Boston

Red Sox. Two iconic hard-nosed competitors, with completely different DNA, were connected by baseball. And a bitter team rivalry.

At the dawn of this golden age, baseball had just moved west, transplanting the interborough rivalry of the New York Giants and Brooklyn Dodgers to two laid-back cities 400 miles apart, San Francisco and Los Angeles. Eight years later Giants pitcher Juan Marichal pounded Dodger catcher Johnny Roseboro over the head with a baseball bat. Voila — the rivalry survived the cross-country migration. Northern and Southern Californians are trained to dislike each other anyway, so the rivalry stuck and grew and remains to this day. But it's a ritualistic rivalry. At the end of the game, the series, the season, it's all forgotten.

Boston and New York is a different matter. It's a birthright rivalry. You're not allowed to not care. It's religious, it's sectarian, and it goes back to the Old Testament or at least 1920 when young Babe Ruth ("The Sultan of Swat") was sold from Boston to New York for $125,000, unleashing a cottage industry of "Curse of the Bambino" mythology. The Yankees and Red Sox will never move—it's an East Coast thing—and so the rivalry is forever and ever. Amen.

**The '60s and '70s were the pre-Moneyball era,** when the important opinions came from managers, not computers. A career baseball man—like Earl Weaver- played in, coached, managed, or scouted 250 games a year for 40 years. That's 10,000 games in a lifetime, give or take, out of which came a headstrong point of view. Manager Hank Bauer, a former Marine, and Al Lopez, a former big league catcher—these were men from the trenches, men you didn't cross. Volcanic one moment, charming the next, these were the last of the foot soldiers turned generals. And what do we do with Casey Stengel, beloved New York manager who was really from Glendale, California? A face with a thousand lines whose rambling speeches were straight from Lewis Carroll and yet, somehow, he handled the grand collection of Yankee egos from Mantle to Maris, from Ford to Berra to Raschi, with the lightest of touch. Just look at Stengel's face. He is the Professor, the clown, the Hall of Famer. Of all the managers, Leo Durocher was the most colorful, but together big league managers comprise a rogues' gallery—when playing a "hunch" had more credibility than running numbers through a laptop pre-programmed with the laws of baseball's statistical probability. Leo? Computers? He'd have said, "You're due, pal. The guy's short-arming garbage up there, so pick something out you like and tattoo the s.o.b." (Translation: "The pitcher's tired. Get a hit.")

Managers were men, like the players, who fought, cursed, drank, and sometimes chased women. Once in the minor leagues, I remember trying to sneak into my assigned hotel after curfew and running into my manager trying to work a woman into the elevator. He and I pretended we didn't see each other (I took the stairs), but it shocked me. It was like seeing your

## Jackie Robinson, Ebbets Field, April 1956

**LEFT** It was a "Camera Day" at Ebbets Field and the ball players posed. Neil got a photo of Jackie Robinson!

**LINKS** „Kamera-Tag" in Ebbets Field, und Neil schießt ein Foto von Jackie Robinson in dessen letzter Saison!

**CI-CONTRE** Jour de la photographie à Ebbets Field: les joueurs prennent la pose et Neil obtient une photo de Jackie Robinson!

father with another woman. But he wasn't my father, I don't even know if he was married, and, as I snuck up the stairway, I prayed that my manager would score because we were on a losing streak and it might relax him. Besides, if he got the woman, he'd probably forget he caught me breaking curfew.

A little-known unwritten rule of professional baseball at any level is that players are not allowed to drink in the hotel bar. That is the exclusive domain of the manager and coaches. Was it fear that drinking together would create bonds that players and managers should not have? Or, as I've always suspected, was it a fear that a manager and a player might find themselves putting their best moves on the same woman — a scenario with no possible happy ending.

These managers had paid dues a hundred times over, spent their lives on the road, worn out their wives, their children, and their livers. They look like old Indian chiefs—our version of Sitting Bull, Crazy Horse, and Geronimo. Hank Bauer, Ralph Houk, Charlie Grimm — let them have the hotel bar, after all, I'll find the dive down the street.

Baseball is not a metaphor for life. It's not a metaphor for anything. In fact, it's nothing like life at all, which is part of its appeal. In life, you run out of time. In baseball, you don't. Life has a clock ticking—baseball doesn't. If you strike out in life, you may never get another shot. In baseball, you're back at the plate in a couple innings. And, if we fail to win at season's end—as all but one team will do—no problem. "Wait till next year" gets us through the winter, to spring training, to new grass ... to new hope.

**On July 20, 1969, two things happened.** I went one for four playing second base for the Stockton Ports against the Lodi Crushers, an Oakland A's farm team. The other thing that night was the game was interrupted for ten minutes to broadcast Neil Armstrong's first step on the moon. We were in the field, I remember, as over the tinny P.A. system came "One small step for man ..." and I turned to our pitcher, Winston Presley, from Compton, and said, "This is something, eh?" And he just pointed up at the moon, which was full and luminous that night, and said, "No way a man's really up there. It's all bullshit." The umpire called for the game to continue, I told Winnie to "throw strikes and keep the ball down and get this thing over with," so we could find a bar in Lodi before it was too late, and the game went on.

Of course even then, in the late '60s in California, Winston Presley would have had a hard time getting a drink in Lodi. He was black, and the Lodi players all lived in our apartment complex in Stockton 20 miles away. They were too uncomfortable in Lodi, yet this was only an hour's drive from San Francisco, the hot spot of radical politics in America. This was also the apartment complex from which we watched Bobby Kennedy's assassination on television, hours after a game, two weeks removed from having seen him give a speech at an election rally across the street.

These juxtapositions were the molecular structure of the air you breathed in the '60s and '70s. An age in which Tiny Tim became a star, while John Coltrane was playing his ass off on a Baltimore striphouse catwalk. An age of Norman Mailer and Jackie Susann, Nixon and Warhol, Ali and Mary Poppins. On one channel Adam Clayton Powell, and on the next channel Laugh-In, and the next channel the My Lai massacre. Stokely Carmichael, Betty Friedan, General Westmoreland, and Snoopy — no wonder everyone was taking drugs. Except in professional baseball.

Not until the end of this golden age did drugs begin creeping in, at first for recreation and then to enhance performance. Speed, of course, didn't count — who's to fault a player for popping a "greenie" or two after an 18-hour bus ride that dumps you on the field to play a double-header in Little Rock on a 100-degree August afternoon? But coke? Something for junkies. Weed? Something for hippies. Steroids? Unheard of. This was all to change, but not quite yet.

This was a game ruled with an iron fist by the owners, a game whose superstars had off-season jobs selling cars and shilling appliances. Mickey Mantle made $30,000 the year he won baseball's triple crown. The following year Mantle's salary doubled.

**Today, we live in an age when .280 hitters sign $50 million multi-year contracts.** Willie Mays made $100,000 in '66. Contemporary star Alex Rodriguez's agreement guarantees him a quarter billion for ten years. Mays and Mantle, if playing today, would own the team.

It all changed in '69 when Curt Flood refused to be traded and became the Rosa Parks of baseball. Eventually, through an arbitration system established in the early 1970s, the hated reserve clause (under which players had a lifetime obligation to their original employer) was killed, freeing them to go to the highest bidder after five years with a single team. Fans cried foul, but a great injustice was corrected, and gradually baseball changed.

Throughout the '70s the game stayed pure, even though the 1960s sensibility crept into the game in small ways. Facial hair appeared and baseball caps perched precariously on Afros, colorful and wild. Brawling teams like the brilliant Oakland A's of the early '70s seemed to confirm that social chaos and change would not affect the quality of play. Oakland players fought among themselves incessantly, then walked onto the field and won three World Series in a row. They had a pitcher named Catfish, a pitcher named Blue Moon, and one named Vida Blue. And Reggie and Rudy and Campy and ...

Neil Leifer was there, not just for the World Series games but for the glorious banality of everyday baseball. The greatest ballplayers who ever lived played to both packed and empty stadiums. It's a game played every day and, unlike pro football, baseball doesn't wait till Sunday afternoon, just 16 times a year. It doesn't exist as a product of television and the concomitant hype.

No, it happens every day, 162 times a year, not counting spring training and playoffs. Sometimes 50,000 people are watching and sometimes 1,500.

This casual dailiness of the game of baseball, at once the fastest and slowest of all sports, is a game in which no clock is ticking. There is no marking off a quarter. "The game isn't over till it's over," Yogi Berra is famous for saying. The idea in baseball is that hope springs eternal, creating great relaxed spaces of time. Because there's time between plays, time in the dugout, time to chat with the opposing first baseman as you lead off the bag, time in the clubhouse, time on the bus trips, time during endless rain delays, the game has rhythms and spaces that need filling, and language becomes the natural thing to fill it with.

**The game of baseball has its own lingo.** Drinking after a game was referred to as "hitting the cocktail circuit" — later shortened to "circuit" as in "You hitting the circuit tonight, 'cause you ain't hit anything else in a month?"

The art of throwing a pitch near a batter's head in order to force him to hit the dirt — without actually hitting him in the head — is a glorious and potentially lethal tradition with its own thesaurus. It has been known as a "knockdown pitch," for obvious reasons, but also the gentler "brushback" as if you can be brushed by a 90-mile-an-hour fastball. In the golden age, it frequently went by the most poetic and misleading of phrases: "chin music." Yeah, right, that's what Bob Gibson and Don Drysdale were throwing at my chin — music.

The fastball itself — variously called "smoke" or "heat" or "gas" or, bizarrely, "cheese," as in "Set him up outside with cheese on the black, waste a hook, then throw some gas in his kitchen." Translation unnecessary, but to the uninitiated it means "Fastball on the outside corner followed by a breaking ball not in the strike zone to entice the batter to swing at a bad pitch, topped off by another fastball, this one inside, right under the hitter's hands."

A home run is called many things, from the obvious "four bagger" of the early days to the postmodern "yard" wherein "He hit it out of the ball yard" turned into "He went yard." But in the golden age, in the '60s and '70s, there were three glorious phrases for the home run. One was "dinger," which I assume was some reference to ringing a bell—and therefore "a lotta dingers in that bandbox" meant a small ballpark inevitably would yield more home runs than a normal-sized park. "I hit the homer, I rang the bell, I took the sledgehammer at the carnival and drove the weight to the very top. I hit a dinger."

A homer also was referred to as "going downtown" — the usage of which would be something like "The guy threw me a cock-high hangin' yellow hammer and I took him downtown," and any eight-year-old knows that's a mediocre curveball, waist high, turned into a dinger. And the delicious notion that the batter could "take" the pitcher downtown — it wasn't just the ball that was hit,

**The first pitch, New York Yankees vs. Los Angeles Dodgers, World Series Game Six, Yankee Stadium, October 18, 1977**

**RIGHT** Still agile at 62, Joe DiMaggio throws out the ceremonial first pitch before the final game of the 1977 World Series.

**RECHTS** Auch mit 62 noch sehr athletisch, wirft Joe DiMaggio den zeremoniellen ersten Ball vor dem letzten Spiel der World Series 1977.

**À DROITE** Encore agile, malgré ses soixante-deux ans, Joe DiMaggio procède à la cérémonie du premier lancer lors de la dernière rencontre des World Series de 1977.

it was the pitcher's ego, statistics, self-esteem, and possibly career, that were redeposited so far beyond the fence that they were, well, downtown. Catch a bus, get out of town, you and that lousy pitch you threw are out of here.

Lastly, a home run was described with the satisfying and somehow rural expression "long tater." (Long potato? A yam? A dinger as a yam?) Often shortened just to "tater," as in "He turned on that cheese and jacked him a tater." Enough said.

The affectionate nickname that people from Brooklyn had for their almost always hapless Dodgers was Bums. Dem (Brooklyn) Bums. When the Dodgers moved to L.A. in '58 they were never referred to as Bums again. The movie stars came out, and a year later the Dodgers won the World Series, something that had taken the first half of the century to achieve in Brooklyn.

**"Dem Bums" had a passionate fan in young Neil Leifer,** who grew up in a housing project on the lower East Side, the "real" lower East Side. He was the son of a postal worker, and a great baseball fan. Neil lived a short subway ride from the Giants' Polo Grounds, Yankee Stadium, and the Dodgers' Ebbets Field. He went to all the games but knew early on that if you were a Dodger, hating the Yankees accompanied the commitment. It was tribal. His hero was Dodgers shortstop Pee Wee Reese because he thought Reese was the shortest player in the league and Neil was the shortest kid on his block. Neil's father was a Giants fan because their third baseman, Sid Gordon, was Jewish. Baseball gave them something else to fight about.

As a 12 year-old, Neil Leifer joined the Camera Club of the Henry Street Settlement near where he lived. A Russian émigré taught the neighborhood kids how to take pictures. Once a week, each kid was given a roll of film and a DeJur twin lens reflex camera, and instructed to come back next week to process the photographs. By 13, Neil was going by subway to the ballgames, and by 15 trying to sell a photo here and there, mostly to Dell Sports publications. Leifer began looking at his beloved sport through a lens and the world began seeing baseball and its heroes in ways they'd never been seen before.

Early in his career, Leifer became aware of something I have known and have included in many of my films: The essence of sports isn't about the defining moments of action ... it's about the time we spend *between* the moments of action. It's not about the big play. It's about everything else.

At age 17 Leifer cajoled a press pass from Dell Sports to cover the 1960 World Series, between the Yankees and the Pirates. *Sports Illustrated* agreed to process Neil's film in return for getting a first look at it. In those days there was no photographers' well, no privileged seating. You hung from the press box, sharing the omniscient view with the writers and principal overhead television camera — or you crouched on concrete in an aisle and hoped nobody hit you over the head with a beer bottle for obstructing their view. Neil felt

he needed a professional camera, so he could compete with the 'Big Boys' at *SI*. The problem was he didn't have $450 and neither did his father. Neil badgered his dad until he agreed to purchase the Nikon F with motordrive and make the 24 payments. Abraham Leifer had never bought anything on credit and was very proud he had no outstanding loans or credit bills. Neil promised to make all the payments from money he made delivering sandwiches for the mid-Manhattan Stage Deli. His father grumbled that it would take his son years to repay the loan.

Veteran *Sports Illustrated* photographers John Zimmerman, Hy Peskin, and Marvin Newman were covering the Series for *SI* when kid Leifer showed up, looking for his own aisle to crouch in. Yogi got to second base, Leifer aimed his new camera with long lens, and bingo — Yogi was picked off and Neil had the perfect angle. *Sports Illustrated* bought it and ran it full-page color! They paid $300. Game two — the Mick (Mickey Mantle) homered and as he entered the dugout, Leifer snapped the moment. The picture sold and ran the next day. Another $150. Neil paid off his dad in full, quit delivering sandwiches, and a career was born.

In subsequent years he would take the most famous boxing photograph of all time — Muhammed Ali standing over the fallen Sonny Liston in Lewiston, Maine, waving his fist, taunting his fallen opponent — as well as countless other unforgettable images from the Sweet Science. He placed cameras high above the boxing ring and with a strobe caught the fallen Cleveland Williams, flat on his back, a remarkable image made more so by the accompanying image of the Ali left hook that put him there, a photo Leifer shot ringside milliseconds earlier. His anticipation, and/or luck, was magnificent.

Football, basketball, the Olympic Games, he's put scores of images into our collective consciousness.

"But baseball is the hardest game to photograph," Leifer says. "It's just waiting, waiting, waiting." Which is probably why it's the best game to write about. All that waiting. Fans have time to talk to each other, even rival players talk to each other. What are they talking about at first base? In the dugout? On the mound? Well, I tried to address that question in *Bull Durham*. But all that talk? How civilized. Until it's not, like every 95-mile-an-hour-fastball in tight on the batter's fists or line drive ripped at the third baseman's feet.

"When it's fast, after the waiting, it's the fastest game," Leifer says, "which is why it's so difficult. I had all my cameras aimed at the great Brooks Robinson at third base for an entire game—and nobody hit a ball to third."

"Even a terrible boxing match can produce great pictures," he says, "but a great baseball game may produce no pictures at all."

Which brings us back to the moments between the action. In what other sport do we care what happens between the plays? In between golf shots, it's all the same. A time out in basketball? A huddle in football? Baseball is all between the lines, in both senses of the term.

Look at "Opening Day, April 10, 1961," at old Griffith Stadium in D.C. Young JFK with his Vice President Lyndon Johnson, also flanked by Senators Mike Mansfield and Everett Dirksen, and Defense Secretary Robert McNamara, watch a popup. Is anything less interesting in sports than a pop foul? But here in this image are five of the most powerful men

in the country, before the Vietnam War has taken root, before free love and Woodstock and Kent State, when all that mattered, for a moment at least, was will this pop foul be caught.

And in another image, Sinatra, a young Mia Farrow, and Leo Durocher, dapper and retired, relax at Dodger Stadium. Stars watching Hall of Famers. How many lawyers, publicists, team reps, and agents would have to be contacted before a picture like that could be taken today? And what about the players? Forget it.

In the golden age, if a photographer wanted a picture of a star player, he simply asked. "You wanted to take a picture of Mantle, you just went to batting practice and waited till he was done and then you said 'Excuse me, Mr. Mantle, could you give me five minutes?' and more often than not they'd give you whatever you needed." It involved a simple 'yes' or expletive 'no,' not a complex multilayered task. Those days are long gone. A photo session with Mantle today would require weeks of negotiation with a cabal of representatives.

**But the photographs in this book take us back to when baseball was, if not pure, certainly innocent.** We forgave their drinking. We loved their brawling. We pretended we didn't know about their womanizing. They wore the name of our city on their chests and so we believed they cared about us and if that was an illusion, then give us our illusions. The ballplayers played hard, they signed autographs for free, their bodies were their own — and they had identifiable faces. They were our team. Some for life. Mickey Mantle was a Yankee. So was DiMaggio. Johnny Bench was a Red and Brooks Robinson was an "O" for life. Fidelity on the field.

So it's not the same now. We all know that. And we know that big money has changed players, given them a sense of privilege and entitlement that separates them from us. They haven't looked like us for a while and they no longer want to talk to us. I don't know who they are anymore, or whom they play for. It's hard to memorize the names on your team if the door to the clubhouse is a revolving door.

The guys Leifer photographed are the guys I know, the guys I aspired to be. What he captured is more than just their faces. It's the way they lounged, the way they stood in the on-deck circle, the way they crouched in the infield, or chased down a fly ball in the alley.

Their body language was more distinctive than a signature — Mantle's autograph could be forged, but nobody could fake the way he trotted out to center field, or the way he struck out. It was beyond imitation. You didn't need

# "Baseball is 90% mental—the other half is physical."
## —Yogi Berra

numbers, uniforms, or programs to tell the gods apart—and Leifer found the iconic signature of each and caught it on film.

For example, Bob Gibson's follow-through, leaping off the mound, challenging the hitter even after the pitch has been released, as if to say "I will not only beat you, I will dominate you."

The whippy motion of Don Drysdale, his right hand flying, his back turned to the plate, is like no other.

Juan Marichal's acrobatic leg kick is as improbable as it is unique.

Henry Aaron, thin, relaxed, coiled, waits for a pitch.

Roberto Clemente, even in still photographs, is always in motion. He's off balance, he's unorthodox, he's fluid, he's the athlete.

Leifer followed the great Clemente and produced volumes of images of the Hall of Famer. The greatest right-handed hitter since World War II, he also possessed perhaps the strongest arm of all time, and we see him at work and waiting to go to work. Clemente in the locker room, Clemente getting a rubdown, Clemente lounging, Clemente signing autographs, Clemente in his hotel room. He has the face of a Greek god, this Puerto Rican by way of the Pittsburgh Pirates. He was a young man discovered by the Dodgers and traded when he was in the minor leagues. Years later he volunteered to fly to Managua, Nicaragua, to help distribute food and medical supplies to the devastated survivors of a tremendous earthquake. The plane crashed on takeoff, and Clemente's brilliant career came to an end. He had 3,000 hits, a lifetime average of .317, and a humanity that inspired the Baseball Hall of Fame to waive its six-year waiting period for eligibility. He was inducted immediately. And the days of the golden age were numbered.

**Leifer snapped the images that stand for a career.** You see Mays laugh, Aaron smile, and Gil Hodges flash his signature broad grin. And even a not-so-crazy Jimmy Piersall, flashing teeth from ear to ear, as he smashes the ball in batting practice. At once you're reminded that these are men playing a boys' game. For a moment, the tough Hank Bauer sticks out his tongue, Billy Martin looks like a choirboy, and Reggie flips Billy over his back, goofing like eight-year-olds, and we recall why we like baseball.

These are part of the record of a golden age from a photographer who knows that the moments before and after the action hold the story.

Leifer gave us all sides and complexions of baseball. The action and the suspended quiet moments all without auto-focus. All without digital. When the center fielder crashed into the fence, Leifer caught it with his 600-millimeter lens, manually focused as the action unfolded. There're no second take here. There's just the work of a great sports photographer hanging out in America's national pastime ... when it still was America's national pastime.

These Neil Leifer portraits of baseball connect us not just to the game

but to our fathers, to our childhood, to memories so private that they aren't otherwise articulated. Your first mitt, the baseball you tied inside your mitt to give it shape, your first organized game, and the time a fellow nine-year-old threw a 30-mile-an-hour fastball by you and the humiliation you felt dragging the bat back to the bench, assuaged only by your first hit—a 20-hop ground ball that got past diving infielders. And suddenly you recall the moment you first laid eyes on your baseball hero. And years later you are older and you realize your gods are human, and there is mortality ... but not in baseball. Leifer's photographs allow for a suspension of disbelief. He sees the game we feel and gives us images that soothe us and stir us. Through these pictures "you can go home again."

Do I exaggerate? Not a bit. That's where these photographs take me, and I suspect, many others. And that is their gift, a gift that even my friend Neil may not fully appreciate.

### The hands of a Cincinnati Red, 1962

**LEFT** Marshall McLuhan wrote that *"we shape our tools, and then our tools shape us."* Two hands gripping a bat express the batter's delicate balance between relaxed anticipation of the pitch and the violent motion of swinging to make solid contact.

**LINKS** Marshall McLuhan schrieb: „Wir formen unsere Werkzeuge, und dann formen unsere Werkzeuge uns." Zwei Hände, die das Schlagholz umfassen, stehen für den schwie-

rigen Balanceakt des Schlagmannes, zugleich entspannt auf den Wurf zu warten und kraftvoll auszuholen, um den Ball ordentlich zu treffen

**CI-CONTRE** Marshall McLuhan a écrit: « Nous forgeons nos outils et, à leur tour, ils nous transforment. » Deux mains agrippent une batte. Elles expriment l'équilibre délicat que doit trouver le batteur entre l'attente du lancer, détendue, et le mouvement violent nécessaire pour propulser la balle.

### Leifer on assignment at Comiskey Park

**OPPOSITE** Young Neil Leifer shoots from the bleachers using a 4,000 mm lens, custom-made for *Life* magazine.

**GEGENÜBER** Von den Bleachers aus fotografiert der junge Neil Leifer mit einem eigens für die Illustrierte

*Life* angefertigten 4000-Millimeter-Objektiv.

**PAGE CI-CONTRE** Neil Leifer photographie depuis les tribunes grâce à un objectif de 4000 mm, fait sur commande pour le magazine *Life*.

# EIN GOLDENES ZEITALTER: BASEBALL IN DEN '60ern UND '70ern

## —Einleitung von Ron Shelton

Zur selben Zeit, da Martin Luther King aus dem Gefängnis in Birmingham seine Briefe schrieb, als JFK und sein Bruder niedergeschossen wurden, als Erfolgsmeldungen aus Vietnam und flaggenbedeckte Särge feste Bestandteile unserer TV-Nachrichten und Jimi und Janis, freie Liebe, Kent State und Bürgerrechtsmärsche nach Selma, Alabama, unser täglich Brot waren – zur selben Zeit gab es ein Paralleluniversum, das von diesen Ereignissen kaum berührt wurde: das goldene Zeitalter des Baseball.

**Wie meist in goldenen Zeitaltern wussten wir vermutlich gar nicht, dass wir in einem lebten.** Das merkt man erst, wenn es vorüber ist. Aber ich weiß es. Ich verdiente meinen Lebensunterhalt als Spieler, als „Eigentum" der Baltimore Orioles. Der Vietnamkrieg war während der Busfahrten unseres Teams oder in den Hotels in Little Rock, Amarillo oder Louisville niemals ein Thema – es schien ihn gar nicht zu geben. Für Baseballspieler zählten damals und zählen heute nur zwei Dinge.

Das eine ist ihre Spielstatistik, denn danach werden sie beurteilt. Jeder Schlagmann weiß: Wenn er bislang nur mit einem von sechs Versuchen erfolgreich war, dann geht's beim nächsten Schlag um den Unterschied zwischen .143 und .286. Zwei aus sieben bedeutet .286 – das weiß man, sobald der Ball durch das Innenfeld fliegt und man in Richtung First Base läuft.

Das Zweite ist der Drang, mit einer Frau ins Bett zu steigen. Die Jungs jagten die Mädchen, die Mädchen die Jungs, und meist musste man gar nicht groß jagen. Statistiken und Weiber, Zahlen und Frauen, von Bar zu Bar, von Stadion zu Stadion – es war eine endlose Reise: schlagen, punkten, einen heißen Fastball werfen, das Spiel machen, bei den Frauen Erfolg haben – auf immer und ewig dasselbe. Amen.

Die Kathedrale namens Baseball kannte keine Attentate, kein Vietnam, keine Protestmärsche. Es zählte nur eines: das Spiel.

Durch Neil Leifers Augen sehen wir die Schönheit des Baseball in den 60ern und 70ern – den besten Jahren, die es je gab für dieses Spiel. Überall in seinen Fotos begegnen wir den Göttern: Mantle, Mays, Clemente, Koufax … Und sie sehen aus wie wir, nur besser. Das sind keine hormongestärkten Muskelprotze. Sie sind häufig auch nicht gerade groß – Henry Aaron war zierlich, Willie Mays war klein. Und Denny McLain? Das ist der untersetzte Typ, der in der Lounge des Holiday Inn die B3-Hammond-Orgel spielt. Er ist übrigens auch der letzte Pitcher, der 30 Spiele gewann.

Das Spiel war anders damals. Es war besser. Und das ist keine Nostalgie, das ist Fakt, oder wie Casey Stengel sagte: „Du kannst es ja nachschlagen" – aber wenn man dies tat, stellte man fest, dass Casey die Zeile bei James Thurber gestohlen hatte. Aber schließlich ist ein Steal ja okay im Baseball.

Helden gab es überall – wir hatten McCovey, Mathews und Maury Wills. Sogar Unsterbliche wie Ted Williams und Stan Musial spielten bis in die 60er hinein. Und die beiden Robinsons, Frank und Brooks, spielten zusammen

in keiner geringeren Mannschaft als den Baltimore Orioles. Die hatten 1971 vier Spieler in ihren Reihen, die 20 Spiele gewonnen hatten. Man muss sich die Namen aus jenen Tagen auf der Zunge zergehen lassen – Gibby, Reggie, Pops, Maz, Yaz, Yogi. Der Vorname reichte völlig aus. Thurman Munson, ein Mann aus dem Mittleren Westen, spielte für die New York Yankees, und Bill „Spaceman" Lee, ein Sozialist aus Südkalifornien, für die Boston Red Sox. Zwei Ikonen, zwei abgebrühte Konkurrenten mit absolut unterschiedlicher DNA kamen durch den Baseball miteinander in Verbindung. Und durch die bittere Rivalität ihrer Teams.

Als das goldene Zeitalter anbrach, war der Baseball gerade nach Westen gezogen, die Stadtteilrivalität zwischen den New York Giants und den Brooklyn Dodgers fand ihr Gegenstück in zwei unverkrampften, 650 Kilometer voneinander entfernten Städten, San Francisco und Los Angeles. Acht Jahre später zog Giants-Pitcher Juan Marichal dem Dodger-Fänger Johnny Roseboro einen Baseballschläger über den Kopf. Voilà – die Rivalität hatte auch die Wanderung nach Westen überlebt. Da die Menschen aus Nord- und aus Südkalifornien ohnehin dazu erzogen werden, einander nicht zu mögen, setzte sich die Rivalität fest, wuchs und besteht bis auf den heutigen Tag. Aber sie ist so etwas wie ein Ritual. Am Ende des Spiels, der Meisterschaft, der Saison ist alles vergessen.

Mit Boston und New York ist das anders. Da geht es um angestammte Rechte. Das darf einem nicht egal sein. Die Rivalität ist religiös, sektiererisch und geht zurück bis auf das Alte Testament oder zumindest bis 1920, als der junge Babe Ruth („Der Sultan des Schlages" oder auch „Bambino" genannt) für 125 000 Dollar von Boston nach New York verkauft wurde, was das nicht enden wollende Ammenmärchen vom „Fluch des Bambino" auslöste (wonach die Red Sox nie wieder die World Series gewinnen würden). Die Yankees und die Red Sox werden sich nie ändern – das ist nun mal so an der Ostküste –, und so wird auch diese Rivalität bis in alle Ewigkeit bestehen bleiben. Amen.

**Die 60er und 70er waren die Jahrzehnte vor dem großen Geld,** als wichtige Dinge noch von Trainern und nicht von Computern entschieden wurden. Ein Baseballprofi wie Earl Weaver war 40 Jahre lang in 250 Spielen pro Jahr als Spieler, Coach, Trainer oder Talentsucher aktiv. Das macht im Laufe eines Lebens 10 000 Spiele, und das führt schon zu durchaus eigenwilligen Ansichten. Trainer Hank Bauer, ein Ex-Marine, und Al Lopez, ein früherer Fänger der Spitzenklasse, hatten alles in vorderster Linie durchlebt, das waren Männer, mit denen man sich besser nicht anlegte. Mal aufbrausend, im nächsten Augenblick wieder voller Charme, waren sie die letzten Infanteristen, aus denen Generale wurden. Und wie war das mit Casey Stengel, dem beliebten Trainer der New York Yankees, der in Wahrheit aus Glendale, Kalifornien, stammte? Ein Gesicht voller Falten, weitschweifige Reden, die direkt von Lewis Carroll hätten stammen können – und doch, irgendwie

## New York Mets Spring Training, Al Lang Field, March 1967

**LEFT** New York Mets coach Yogi Berra (foreground) joins Mets players in the spring training ritual of physical conditioning to work off those extra pounds put on during a winter spent hunting and fishing.

**LINKS** Yogi Berra (vorn), Trainer der New York Mets, leistet seinen Spielern im Frühjahrstraining beim Workout Gesellschaft, um die Extrapfunde vom Jagen und Fischen im Winter loszuwerden.

**CI-CONTRE** Le coach des New York Mets, Yogi Berra (au premier plan), se joint à ses joueurs lors de la traditionnelle remise en forme au début de l'Entraînement de printemps. Il tente de perdre quelques kilos superflus amassés lors d'un hiver passé à la pêche et à la chasse.

führte er die Yankee-Stars von Mantle bis Maris, von Ford bis Berra und Raschi mit absolut leichter Hand. Er ist der Professor, der Clown, der Mann für die Hall of Fame.

Von allen Trainern war Leo Durocher der farbigste, aber insgesamt waren die Toptrainer schon ein Haufen Spitzbuben – zu einer Zeit, da glaubwürdiger war, wer seinem Bauchgefühl folgte, statt Zahlen in einen Laptop einzugeben, der mit den Gesetzen der statistischen Wahrscheinlichkeit im Baseball gefüttert ist. Leo und Computer? Er hätte gesagt: „Jetzt bist du dran, Junge. Der Kerl da wirft doch nur noch Kleinzeug, also lass dir was einfallen, mach den Hundesohn zur Schnecke." (Soll heißen: „Der Pitcher ist müde. Jetzt triff den Ball mal ordentlich.")

Die Trainer – das waren Männer, die ebenso wie die Spieler kämpften, fluchten, tranken und manchmal auch Jagd auf Frauen machten. Einmal, als ich noch in einer der unteren Mannschaften spielte, versuchte ich, mich nach dem Zapfenstreich in mein Hotel zu stehlen. Dabei stieß ich auf meinen Trainer, der eine Frau in den Fahrstuhl zu bugsieren versuchte. Wir taten so, als hätten wir einander nicht gesehen (ich nahm die Treppe), aber ich war schockiert. Das war so, als hätte man seinen Vater mit einer anderen Frau erwischt. Aber er war nicht mein Vater, und während ich die Treppe hinaufschlich, betete ich, dass er Erfolg haben möge, denn wir hatten gerade eine Serie von Niederlagen hinter uns, und vielleicht würde ihn das ja entspannen. Und außerdem würde er, wenn er die Frau bekam, möglicherweise vergessen, dass er mich nach dem Zapfenstreich erwischt hatte.

Eine kaum bekannte ungeschriebene Regel im Profibaseball ist, dass Spieler an der Hotelbar keinen Drink nehmen dürfen. Die Hotelbar ist ausschließlich dem Trainer und seinem Stab vorbehalten. Fürchtete man, dass gemeinsames Trinken Bindungen zwischen Spielern und Trainern erzeugen könnte, die es besser nicht gab? Oder fürchtete man, wie ich stets vermutete, dass ein Trainer und ein Spieler möglicherweise dieselbe Frau anmachten – ein Szenario, für das es kein Happy End geben konnte?

Diese Trainer hatten immer und immer wieder ihre Pflicht und Schuldigkeit getan, hatten ihr Leben auf Reisen verbracht, ihre Frauen und Kinder vernachlässigt, ihre Leber ruiniert. Sie sehen aus wie alte Indianerhäuptlinge – unsere Version von Sitting Bull, Crazy Horse und Geronimo. Hank Bauer, Ralph Houk, Charlie Grimm – die Hotelbar sei ihnen gegönnt, ich finde schon weiter unten in der Straße eine Kneipe.

Baseball ist keine Metapher für das Leben. Baseball hat mit dem Leben überhaupt nichts zu tun, und das macht das Spiel so reizvoll. Im wahren Leben wird dir die Zeit knapp, nicht so im Baseball. Die Uhr des Lebens tickt immer weiter – nicht die beim Baseball. Wenn dir im Leben was danebengeht, kriegst du selten eine zweite Chance. Im Baseball bist du schon nach ein paar Innings wieder am Schlag. Und wenn wir am Ende der Saison den Titel nicht gewonnen haben – auch kein Problem: Bis auf eine einzige Mann-

schaft geht das allen so. „Wartet aufs nächste Jahr" – der Spruch hilft uns durch den Winter, ins Frühjahrstraining, auf neuen Rasen … und zu neuer Hoffnung.

**Am 20. Juli 1969 passierten zwei Dinge.** Ich war mit einem von vier Schlagversuchen als Second Baseman der Stockton Ports gegen die Lodi Crushers erfolgreich, ein Nachwuchsteam der Oakland A's. Und außerdem wurde das Spiel an jenem Abend wegen der Übertragung von Neil Armstrongs erstem Schritt auf dem Mond für zehn Minuten unterbrochen. Ich erinnere mich noch: Wir standen auf dem Platz, und als aus dem blechernen Lautsprecher der Satz „That's one small step for man …" ertönte, sagte ich zu Winston Presley, unserem Pitcher aus Compton: „Das ist 'n Ding, nicht?" Er deutete nur auf den Mond und sagte: „Da oben ist doch kein Mensch. Das ist alles Schwachsinn." Als der Schiedsrichter das Spiel wieder freigab, forderte ich Winnie auf, „gute Bälle zu werfen, die Kugel niedrig zu halten und die Sache hinter uns zu bringen", damit wir in Lodi noch eine Bar finden konnten, bevor es zu spät war. Und das Spiel ging weiter.

Natürlich hätte Winston Presley damals sowieso noch Schwierigkeiten gehabt, in Lodi einen Drink zu bekommen. Er war schwarz, und die Spieler aus Lodi wohnten alle in unserem Apartmentkomplex in Stockton, über 30 Kilometer entfernt. Sie fühlten sich in Lodi nicht wohl in ihrer Haut, obwohl Lodi nur eine gute Autostunde von San Francisco entfernt ist, dem Herd radikaler Politik in Amerika. Es war derselbe Apartmentkomplex, in dem wir, ein paar Stunden nach einem Spiel, im Fernsehen die Ermordung Bobby Kennedys verfolgten, nur zwei Wochen nachdem wir ihn bei einer Wahlkampfrede auf der anderen Straßenseite gesehen hatten.

Dieses Nebeneinander unterschiedlicher Ereignisse prägte das Klima in den 60ern und 70ern. Es war die Zeit, in der Tiny Tim ein Star wurde, während sich John Coltrane auf dem Laufsteg eines Striplokals in Baltimore den Arsch aufriss. Die Zeit von Norman Mailer und Jackie Susann, Nixon und Warhol, Ali und Mary Poppins. Auf einem TV-Kanal Adam Clayton Powell, auf einem anderen *Laugh-In* und auf dem nächsten das My-Lai-Massaker. Stokely Carmichael, Betty Friedan, General Westmoreland und Snoopy – kein Wunder, dass alle Welt Drogen nahm.

Außer im Profibaseball. Erst gegen Ende dieses goldenen Zeitalters schlichen sich die Drogen ein, anfangs zur Entspannung, dann aber auch zur Leistungssteigerung. Speed zählte natürlich nicht – wer will schon einem Spieler vorwerfen, nach einer 18-stündigen Busfahrt ein oder zwei „Greenies" einzuwerfen, bevor er auf einem Platz in Little Rock ausgeladen wird, wo er nachmittags im August bei fast 40 Grad zwei Partien hintereinander spielen soll? Aber Kokain? Etwas für Junkies. Marihuana? Etwas für Hippies. Nie gehört. Das sollte sich alles ändern, aber noch nicht sogleich.

Baseball war ein Spiel, das von den Eigentümern mit harter Hand be-

herrscht wurde, ein Spiel, dessen Superstars außerhalb der Saison Autos oder Groschenartikel verkauften. In dem Jahr, als er die Triple Crown gewann, verdiente Mickey Mantle 30 000 Dollar. Im Jahr darauf wurde sein Gehalt verdoppelt.

**Heute leben wir in einer Zeit, da .280-Schlagleute mehrjährige Verträge über 50 Millionen Dollar abschließen.** Wenn May und Mantle heute spielten, gehörte ihnen das Team.

Der Wandel begann 1969, als Curt Flood sich weigerte, verkauft zu werden, und zur Rosa Parks des Baseball wurde. Ein Schiedsgerichtssystem, das in den frühen 70ern eingeführt wurde, sorgte dafür, dass die verhasste Reserveklausel aufgehoben wurde, die besagte, dass die Spieler ihr Leben lang ihrem ersten Arbeitgeber verpflichtet seien. Fortan waren sie frei, nach fünf Jahren bei ein und demselben Team zum höchsten Bieter zu wechseln. Die Fans waren empört, aber dadurch wurde eine große Ungerechtigkeit korrigiert, und nach und nach änderte sich der Baseballsport.

Während der 70er ging es beim Baseball einzig um Baseball, obwohl die gesellschaftlichen Veränderungen der 60er den Baseball durchaus schon in geringem Umfang erreicht hatten. Es gab die ersten Bärte, die ersten Baseballmützen auf Afro-Köpfen. Rüpelhafte Teams wie die brillanten Oakland A's schienen zu bestätigen, dass gesellschaftliches Chaos und gesellschaftlicher Wandel die Qualität des Spiels nicht beeinträchtigten. Die Spieler von Oakland waren untereinander ständig zerstritten, aber dann kamen sie gemeinsam aufs Spielfeld und gewannen dreimal hintereinander die World Series.

Neil Leifer war dabei, nicht nur bei den Spielen der World Series, er fing auch die glorreichen Banalitäten des Baseball ein. Die besten Spieler aller Zeiten spielten sowohl in ausverkauften wie auch in leeren Stadien. Im Gegensatz zum Football wird Baseball jeden Tag gespielt, nicht nur 16-mal im Jahr am Sonntagnachmittag. Baseball ist kein Produkt des Fernsehens und des damit einhergehenden Wirbels. Nein, Baseball passiert jeden Tag, 162-mal im Jahr, Frühjahrstraining und die Entscheidungsspiele nicht eingerechnet. Manchmal schauen 50 000 Leute zu, manchmal 1500.

Baseball, die schnellste, aber auch die langsamste aller Sportarten, ist deswegen von so zwangloser Alltäglichkeit, weil in diesem Spiel keine Uhr tickt. Es gibt keine zeitlich definierten Spielhälften oder -viertel. „Das Spiel ist erst zu Ende, wenn es zu Ende ist", war so ein Satz, den Yogi Berra berühmt machte. Das bedeutet, dass es auf ewig neue Hoffnung gibt, er fing immer wieder zu langen, entspannten Pausen führt. Weil es freie Zeit zwischen den Spielzügen gibt, Zeit auf der Spielerbank, Zeit für einen Schwatz mit dem Gegner, während man sich vom Base wegschleicht, Zeit im Clubhaus, Zeit auf Busreisen, Zeit während endloser Regenpausen – das Spiel hat Rhythmen und Räume, die gefüllt werden müssen, und da wird die Sprache das natürliche Mittel, um sie zu füllen.

> **"A hot dog at the ballgame**
> **beats a steak at the Ritz."**
> —*Humphrey Bogart*

**Baseball hat seinen eigenen Jargon.** Die Sauferei nach dem Spiel nannte man *hitting the cocktail circuit* (etwa: die Kneipenrunde machen), später sprach man nur noch vom *circuit*: „You hitting the circuit tonight, 'cause you ain't hit anything else in a month?" – ein Wortspiel mit dem Verb „to hit", das sowohl „auf den Weg machen" wie auch „treffen" (mit dem Schlagholz) bedeuten kann, also: „Willst (du) dich heute Abend vollaufen lassen, weil du schon einen ganzen Monat lang keinen Ball mehr getroffen hast?"

Die Kunst, einen Ball so nahe wie möglich an den Kopf des Fängers zu werfen, sodass dieser sich auf den Boden fallen lassen muss, ist eine glorreiche und potenziell tödliche Tradition mit einem eigenen Synonymwörterbuch. Man spricht aus naheliegenden Gründen von einem „K. o.-Wurf", aber auch etwas weniger martialisch von einem *brushback* – so als ob man von einem knapp 150 Stundenkilometer schnellen Fastball überhaupt *leicht* berührt werden könnte. Im goldenen Zeitalter benutzte man oft auch den besonders poetischen und besonders irreführenden Ausdruck *chin music*. Ja, wirklich, das war's, womit Bob Gibson und Don Drysdale in Richtung meines Kinns zielten – Musik.

Der Fastball selbst hat ebenfalls eine Vielzahl anderer Namen – „Rauch" (*smoke*) zum Beispiel, „Hitze" (*heat*), „Gas" (*gas*) oder, völlig bizarr, „Käse" (*cheese*), so etwa in folgendem Satz: „Set him up outside with cheese on the black, waste a hook, then throw some gas in his kitchen." Übersetzung überflüssig. Nur für den Laien hier die Bedeutung: „Fastball in die *outside corner*, gefolgt von einem Ball mit Spin außerhalb der Schlagzone, um den Schlagmann zu verleiten, nach einem schlechten Wurf zu schlagen, danach noch ein Fastball, dieser aber *inside*, direkt unter die Hände des Schlagmanns."

Ein Homerun hat ebenfalls eine Vielzahl von Namen, vom naheliegenden *four bagger* (vier Male) der Frühzeit bis zum hochaktuellen *yard*, wobei aus „He hit it out of the ball yard" „He went yard" wurde, was beides nichts anderes bedeutet, als dass der Schlag über den Zaun flog. Im goldenen Zeitalter gab es noch drei glorreiche Bezeichnungen für den Homerun. Die eine war *dinger* – ein Wort, von dem ich annehme, dass es so etwas wie das Läuten einer Glocke ausdrücken sollte –, „ein Haufen *dinger* in der *bandbox*" bedeutete, dass es in einem kleinen Stadion unweigerlich mehr Homeruns gab als in einem normal großen Stadion. „Ich machte den Homer, läutete die Glocke, nahm den Vorschlaghammer und trieb das Gewicht bis ganz nach oben. Ich schlug einen *dinger*."

*Going downtown* (in die Stadt gehen) war eine andere Umschreibung für den Homer und wurde beispielsweise in dieser Formulierung verwendet: „Der Kerl warf mir in Schwanzhöhe einen leicht zu treffenden Ball mit Spin zu – und ich schickte ihn in die Stadt." Die köstliche Vorstellung, dass der Schlagmann den Pitcher *downtown* „schicken" konnte – da war nicht nur der Ball getroffen, sondern da war das Ego des Pitchers, seine Statistiken, mögli-

cherweise sogar seine gesamte Karriere jenseits des Zauns gelandet, also eben in der Stadt.

Schließlich wurde ein Homerun auch noch mit dem Ausdruck *long tater* belegt. Oftmals wurde auch nur die Abkürzung *tater* benutzt, zum Beispiel in diesem Satz: „Er warf diesen Cheese-Ball, und das brachte ihm einen *tater*." Genug davon.

Der liebevolle Spitzname der Menschen in Brooklyn für ihre fast immer glücklosen Dodgers lautete *Bums*, Penner. Nachdem die Dodgers 1958 nach L. A. gezogen waren, wurden sie nie wieder als *Bums* bezeichnet. Die Filmstars kamen ins Stadion, und ein Jahr später gewannen die Dodgers die World Series. In Brooklyn hatten sie dafür ein halbes Jahrhundert gebraucht.

**Ein leidenschaftlicher Anhänger der „Dem Bums" war der junge Neil Leifer,** der in einer Anlage des sozialen Wohnungsbaus an der Lower East Side aufwuchs, der – wahren – Lower East Side. Neil, Sohn eines Postbediensteten, der selbst ein großer Baseballfan war, wohnte nur ein paar Subway-Stationen entfernt von den Polo Grounds der Giants, vom Yankee-Stadion und dem Ebbets Field der Dodgers. Er ging zu allen Spielen, und er wusste schon sehr bald: Für einen wahren Dodger gehörte es ganz einfach dazu, die Yankees zu hassen. Das waren verfeindete Stämme. Sein Held war Dodgers-Shortstop Pee Wee Reese, den er für den kleinsten Spieler der Liga hielt – und er selbst war schließlich der kleinste Junge in der Gegend. Neils Vater war Fan der Giants, weil deren dritter Basemann, Sid Gordon, Jude war. Baseball war also für Vater und Sohn ein herrliches Streitthema.

Mit zwölf wurde Neil Leifer Mitglied des Kamera-Clubs im Henry Street Settlement in der Nähe seiner Wohnung. Ein russischer Emigrant brachte den Kindern aus der Gegend bei, wie man Fotos schoss. Einmal wöchentlich erhielt jedes Kind eine Rolle Film, eine doppellinsige DeJur-Kamera, die aussah wie eine Rolleiflex, und die Order, eine Woche später zum Entwickeln der Bilder wiederzukommen. Mit 13 fuhr Neil mit der Subway zu den Baseballspielen, und als er 15 war, versuchte er, das eine oder andere Foto zu verkaufen, meist an die Zeitschrift *Dell Sports*. Leifer fing an, seinen geliebten Sport durch den Sucher seiner Kamera zu erleben, und für die Welt bedeutete das, dass sie Baseball und seine Helden auf eine ganz andere Art als je zuvor zu sehen bekam.

Schon früh in seiner Karriere wurde Leifer etwas klar, dessen auch ich mir bewusst bin und das in viele meiner Filme eingeflossen ist: Beim Sport geht es nicht in erster Linie um die jeweiligen sportarttypischen Handlungen, sondern um die Zeit, die wir *zwischen* diesen Aktivitäten verbringen. Es geht nicht um den großen Spielzug, es geht um alles andere.

Mit 17 schwatzte Leifer den Leuten von *Dell Sports* ein Presseticket für die World Series 1960 zwischen den Yankees und den Pirates ab. Mit *Sports Illustrated* machte er ein Gegenschäft: Sie entwickelten seine Bilder und

hatten als Gegenleistung als Erste Zugriff darauf. In jenen Tagen gab es keinen Pressegraben und keine speziellen Sitzplätze für die Fotografen. Man hing in der Pressekabine, sah dasselbe wie die Reporter und die Fernsehkamera an der Decke – oder man kauerte auf dem Betonboden eines Tribünenabgangs, dass einem niemand eine Bierflasche auf den Kopf haute, weil er sich angeblich in der Sicht behindert fühlte. Neil wusste, dass er eine Profikamera brauchte, um mit den „Big Boys" von *Sports Illustrated* mithalten zu können. Das Problem war nur, dass er keine 450 Dollar hatte – und sein Vater auch nicht. Neil lag seinem Vater so lange in den Ohren, bis der damit einverstanden war, eine Nikon F mit einem Motor für den automatischen Filmtransport auf 24 Raten zu kaufen. Abraham Leifer hatte nie etwas auf Raten gekauft und war sehr stolz darauf, keine Schulden oder offenen Rechnungen zu haben. Neil versprach, alle Raten mit dem Geld zu bezahlen, das er fürs Ausliefern von Sandwiches beim StageDeli in Midtown Manhattan verdiente. Sein Vater knurrte, der Sohn würde Jahre brauchen, um das Darlehen zurückzuzahlen.

Für *Sports Illustrated* berichteten drei alte Hasen, John Zimmerman, Hy Peskin und Marvin Newman, als Fotografen über die World Series; nun tauchte auch noch Klein-Leifer auf und suchte sich einen eigenen Abgang im Stadion, wo er sich hinhocken konnte. Yogi erreichte das zweite Base, Leifer richtete das Teleobjektiv seiner neuen Kamera auf ihn, und bingo: Yogi wurde von einem *pickoff* erwischt, und Neil saß genau an der richtigen Stelle. *Sports Illustrated* kaufte das Foto und druckte es in Farbe auf einer vollen Seite! Als Honorar gab es 300 Dollar. Spiel zwei: Der große Mickey Mantle machte einen Homerun, und Leifer erwischte ihn just als er zur Spielerbank zurückkam. Wieder ein Bild verkauft, das am nächsten Tag gedruckt wurde. Wieder 150 Dollar. Neil zahlte seinem Vater das Darlehen zurück und hörte auf, Sandwiches auszuliefern. Seine Karriere hatte begonnen.

In den folgenden Jahren schoss er das berühmteste Boxfoto aller Zeiten – es zeigt Muhammad Ali, wie er sich in Lewiston, Maine, über den besiegten Sonny Liston beugt, die Faust schwenkt und seinen Gegner verhöhnt – sowie unzählige weitere unvergessene Bilder der schönen Boxkunst. Er platzierte Kameras hoch über dem Boxring und hielt mithilfe eines Strobolights den zu Boden geschlagenen Cleveland Williams fest, wie er flach auf dem Rücken lag: ein ungewöhnliches Bild, dessen nachhaltiger Eindruck noch durch das Foto von jenem linken Haken verstärkt wurde, mit dem Ali ihn niedergeschlagen hatte – ein Bild, das Leifer Sekundenbruchteile zuvor von seinem Platz am Ring aus geschossen hatte. Seine Fähigkeit, die Dinge vorauszuahnen – und/oder sein Glück –, war fantastisch.

Football, Basketball, die Olympischen Spiele – er hat unser aller Bewusstsein mit Dutzenden von Fotos bereichert.

„Aber Baseball ist am schwersten zu fotografieren", sagt Leifer. „Du musst immer nur warten, warten, warten." Was wahrscheinlich der Grund dafür

## Brooks Robinson, Baltimore Orioles

**LEFT** Enveloped in darkness, the pitcher has tunnel vision as he faces Hall of Famer Brooks Robinson.

**LINKS** Eingehüllt in Dunkelheit, entwickelt der Pitcher einen Tunnelblick, als er dem Hall-of-Fame-Star Brooks Robinson gegenübersteht.

**CI-CONTRE** Le lanceur affronte Brooks Robinson, membre du Temple de la renommée. Il le voit comme au bout d'un long tunnel, enveloppé dans l'obscurité.

## The Green Monster, Boston Red Sox vs. St. Louis Cardinals, World Series game One, Fenway Park, October 4, 1967

**OPPOSITE** Nobody defended Fenway's famed left field wall better than Red Sox Hall of Famer Carl Yastrzemski, whose acrobatic catch robs Curt Flood of a hit.

**GEGENÜBER** Niemand verteidigte die berühmte Wand im Left Field des Fenway Park besser als Hall-of-Fame-Mitglied Carl Yastremski von den Red Sox, dessen akrobatischer Fang hier Curt Flood um einen Erfolg bringt.

**PAGE CI-CONTRE** Personne n'a jamais aussi bien défendu le fameux mur gauche du Fenway Park que le joueur des Red Sox, Carl Yastrzemski, membre du Temple de la renommée. Ici, son arrêt acrobatique empêche Curt Flood de réaliser un coup sûr.

ist, dass dies der Sport ist, über den man am besten schreiben kann. All das Warten. Die Fans haben Zeit, miteinander zu reden, sogar die gegnerischen Spieler reden miteinander. Worüber reden sie am First Base? Worüber auf der Spielerbank? Am Wurfmal? Also, ich habe versucht, das in meinem Film *Bull Durham* zu thematisieren. Aber all das Gerede? Wie zivilisiert. Bis es dann ernst wird – wie jeder Fastball, der mit Tempo 150 knallhart auf die Faust des Schlägers trifft, oder jeder gewaltige *line drive* auf die Füße des Mannes am dritten Base.

„Wenn's schnell wird, nach der Warterei, dann ist es das schnellste Spiel", erklärt Leifer. „Und deshalb ist es so schwer. Ich hatte alle meine Kameras das ganze Spiel über auf den großen Brooks Robinson auf Base drei gerichtet – aber niemand schlug den Ball auf Base drei."

„Sogar von einem schlechten Boxkampf kann man tolle Fotos machen", sagt er, „aber von einem tollen Baseballspiel möglicherweise gar keine."

Womit wir wieder bei den Momenten sind, in denen es keine Action gibt. Nehmen wir die „Saisoneröffnung, 10. April 1961" im alten Griffith-Stadion in Washington. Der junge JFK, sein Vize Lyndon Johnson, dazu die Senatoren Mike Mansfield und Everett Dirksen sowie Verteidigungsminister Robert McNamara, sehen ein *popup*. Es gibt kaum etwas im Sport, das so wenig interessant ist wie ein *popup*-Foul. Aber hier haben wir – bevor der Vietnamkrieg Wurzeln schlug, in der Zeit vor freier Liebe, Woodstock und Kent State – fünf der mächtigsten Männer des Landes im Bild, und in diesem Augenblick ist nur eines wichtig: Wird das Foul geahndet?

Ein anderes Bild: Sinatra und eine junge Mia Farrow, dazu Leo Durocher, entspannen sich im Dodger-Stadion. Stars beim Spiel der Helden aus der Hall of Fame. Mit wie vielen Anwälten, Werbefachleuten, Teambeauftragten und Agenten müsste man sich heutzutage arrangieren, bevor man ein solches Foto aufnehmen könnte? Und die Spieler? Vergiss es.

Wenn ein Fotograf im goldenen Zeitalter ein Foto eines Topspielers machen wollte, fragte er ihn einfach. „Wenn du Mantle fotografieren wolltest, gingst du einfach zum Schlagtraining, wartetest, bis er fertig war, und fragtest dann: ‚Entschuldigung, Mr. Mantle, haben Sie fünf Minuten für mich?', und *fast immer* bekamst du, was du wolltest." Ein einfaches Ja, ein deutliches Nein, aber keine komplizierte, mehrdeutige Aussage. Das war einmal. Um Aufnahmen mit Mantle machen zu können, müsste man heute erst wochenlang mit einem Klüngel von Repräsentanten verhandeln.

**Aber die Fotos in diesem Buch bringen uns zurück in die Zeit, als der Baseball wenn nicht absolut sauber, so doch unschuldig war.** Wir haben den Spielern das Trinken vergeben. Wir liebten ihre Prügeleien. Wir taten so, als wüssten wir nichts über ihre Frauengeschichten. Sie trugen auf der Brust ihrer Trikots den Namen unserer Stadt. Also *glaubten* wir, dass sie sich etwas aus uns machten. Und wenn das eine Illusion war,

dann sollte man uns unsere Illusionen lassen. Die Spieler arbeiteten hart, gaben umsonst Autogramme, ihre Körper gehörten ihnen – und man konnte sie an ihren Gesichtern erkennen. Sie waren unser Team. Manche ein Leben lang. Mickey Mantle war ein Yankee. DiMaggio ebenso. Johnny Bench war ein Red und Brooks Robinson lebenslang ein „O". Treue auf dem Spielfeld.

So ist es heute nicht mehr. Wir alle wissen das. Und wir wissen, dass das große Geld die Spieler verändert hat, in ihnen einen Sinn für Privilegien und Ansprüche weckte, was wiederum zu einer Trennung zwischen ihnen und uns geführt hat. Sie sehen schon seit geraumer Zeit nicht mehr so aus wie wir, und sie wollen auch nicht mehr mit uns reden. Ich weiß nicht mehr, wer sie sind und für wen sie spielen. Es fällt schwer, sich bei diesem ständigen Kommen und Gehen die Spielernamen deiner Mannschaft zu merken.

Die Burschen, die Leifer fotografiert hat, sind die Jungs, die ich kenne, denen ich nachgeeifert habe. Was er einfing, sind nicht nur die Gesichter, es ist die Art, wie sie herumsaßen, wie sie im *on-deck*-Kreis herumstanden und warteten, bis sie als Schlagmann an der Reihe waren, wie sie im Innenfeld hockten oder wie sie einen hohen Ball in der *alley* nachjagten.

Ihre Körpersprache sagte mehr aus als eine Unterschrift. Mantles Autogramm konnte gefälscht sein, aber niemand konnte so wie er ins Center Field traben oder so zum Schlag ausholen wie er. Das entzog sich jeder Nachahmung. Man brauchte keine Rückennummern, Trikots oder Programmhefte, um die Götter auseinanderzuhalten – und Leifer erkannte das Spezifische jeder Einzelnen dieser Ikonen und bannte es auf Film.

Wie zum Beispiel Bob Gibson seine Routine durchzog, vom Wurfmal sprang, den Schlagmann noch nach dem Wurf herausforderte, so als wollte er sagen: „Ich werde dich nicht nur besiegen, ich werde dich dominieren."

Die federnde Bewegung von Don Drysdale, die Rechte in der Luft, den Rücken zum Schlagmal – das gab's nur einmal.

Juan Marichals akrobatischer Beinschlag – ebenso unglaublich wie einzigartig.

Henry Aron, dünn, entspannt, zusammengerollt, wartet auf einen Wurf.

Roberto Clemente – sogar auf Standfotos immer in Bewegung. Aufgeregt, unorthodox, fließend, *der* Athlet.

Leifer beobachtete den großen Clemente und produzierte ganze Bände von Fotos des Stars aus der Hall of Fame. Der bedeutendste Rechtshänder unter den Schlagleuten seit dem Zweiten Weltkrieg besaß vermutlich auch den stärksten Arm aller Zeiten. Wir sehen ihn bei der Arbeit und wie er auf seine Arbeit wartet. Clemente im Umkleideraum, Clemente während einer Massage, Clemente faul herumhängend, Clemente beim Autogrammschreiben, Clemente in seinem Hotelzimmer. Der Puerto Ricaner von den Pittsburgh Pirates mit dem Gesicht eines griechischen Gottes. Als junger Mann war er von den Dodgers entdeckt und verkauft worden, als er in den Minor Leagues spielte. Viele Jahre später, 1972, meldete er sich freiwillig für einen

Flug nach Managua, Nicaragua, um bei der Ausgabe von Lebens- und Arzneimitteln an die verzweifelten Überlebenden eines verheerenden Erdbebens zu helfen. Die Maschine verunglückte beim Abflug, und das war das Ende seiner brillanten Karriere – mit 3000 Schlägen, einer Trefferquote von .317 und einer Menschlichkeit, welche die Hall of Fame veranlasste, die für die Aufnahme vorgesehene Wartezeit von fünf Jahren in seinem Fall aufzuheben. Er wurde sofort aufgenommen. Das goldene Zeitalter näherte sich seinem Ende.

**Leifers schoss die Fotos, die ganze Karrieren symbolisieren.** Man sieht einen lachenden Mays, einen lächelnden Aaron und einen Gil Hodges mit seinem typischen breiten Grinsen. Selbst ein sonst gar nicht so alberner Jimmy Persall lässt seine Zähne beim Schlagtraining von einem Ohr zum anderen blitzen. Mit einem Mal merkt man, dass hier große Jungs spielen. Für einen Augenblick steckt der harte Hank Bauer die Zunge aus, gleicht Billy Martin einem Chorknaben, wirft sich Reggie den Billy über die Schulter, albern wie Achtjährige, und wir wissen wieder, warum wir Baseball lieben.

Diese Bilder sind Teil der Geschichte des goldenen Zeitalters, aufgenommen von einem Fotografen, der weiß, dass die Story in den Augenblicken vor und nach der Action auf dem Spielfeld steckt.

Leifer hat uns alle Seiten und Schattierungen des Baseball gezeigt, die Action und die vorübergehenden stillen Momente – alles ohne Autofokus, alles ohne Digitalkameras. Wenn der Center Fielder in den Zaun knallte, hielt Leifer das mit seinem 600-Millimeter-Objektiv fest, das er währenddessen von Hand scharf stellte. Da gab es keine zweite Chance.

Diese Baseballporträts von Neil Leifer bringen uns nicht nur dem Spiel nahe, sondern auch unseren Vätern, unserer Kindheit – Erinnerungen, die so persönlich sind, dass sie sonst kaum je artikuliert werden. Dein erster Fanghandschuh, dein erstes richtiges Match, der Augenblick, als der Fastball eines anderen Neunjährigen mit Tempo 50 an dir vorbeisauste, wie erniedrigt du dich fühltest, als du mit dem Schlagstock zur Bank zurückschlurftest – ein Gefühl, das erst nach deinem ersten Treffer wieder nachließ, einem Ground Ball, der 20-mal aufsprang, vorbei an den Infieldern, die sich zu Boden warfen. Und plötzlich erinnerst du dich an den Augenblick, in dem du deinen Baseballhelden zum ersten Mal zu Gesicht bekamst. Und Jahre später, inzwischen älter geworden, wird dir klar, dass deine Götter auch nur Menschen sind und dass nichts unsterblich ist … außer im Baseball. Leifers Fotos lassen dich für einen Augenblick an Wunder glauben. Er sieht das Spiel mit unseren Augen und liefert uns Bilder, die uns beruhigen und bewegen. Dank dieser Bilder „kannst du wieder nach Hause gehen".

Ich übertreibe? Keineswegs. Genau dahin bringen mich diese Bilder wieder zurück und viele andere vermutlich ebenso. Und das macht sie zu einem Geschenk, einer Gabe, deren Wert mein Freund Neil möglicherweise gar nicht einmal so richtig zu schätzen weiß.

# L'ÂGE D'OR DU BASEBALL : LES ANNÉES SOIXANTE ET SOIXANTE-DIX

*—Introduction par Ron Shelton*

Lorsque Martin Luther King écrivait ses lettres en prison à Birmingham, lorsque JFK et son frère ont été assassinés, quand le décompte des morts et les cercueils drapés dans la bannière étoilée apparaissaient tous les soirs à la télé, quand Jimi et Janis, la révolution sexuelle, la fac de Kent State et les marches pour les Droits civils à Selma dans l'Alabama, représentaient notre pain quotidien, il existait un univers parallèle que tous ces événements laissaient en grande partie indemne. C'était l'âge d'or du baseball.

**J'imagine que, comme pour la plupart des âges d'or, il faut en voir la fin pour comprendre que c'en était un.** Je le sais. J'ai gagné ma vie grâce à ce sport en étant la « propriété » des Baltimore Orioles. On ne parlait jamais de la guerre lors des trajets en bus ni dans les hôtels de Little Rock, Amarillo ou Louisville – comme si le Vietnam n'avait jamais existé. En fait, à l'époque, deux obsessions menaient les joueurs de baseball par le bout du nez (c'est sans doute toujours le cas).

D'abord les statistiques, parce que c'est la façon dont ils sont jugés. Tous les batteurs savent que s'ils traversent une mauvaise passe, disons à un coup pour six (un coup sûr pour six présences à la batte), la présence à la batte suivante peut faire évoluer la statistique de 0,143 à 0,286. Deux pour sept, c'est 0,286. Vous le savez dès que la balle franchi le champ intérieur et que vous courez vers la première base.

Deuxième obsession des joueurs de baseball : les parties de jambes en l'air. Les mecs pourchassent les filles. Et inversement. La plupart du temps, la « cour » est plutôt rapide. Stats et gonzesses, chiffres et femmes, de bar en bar, de stade en stade : un voyage infini, frapper, marquer, lancer une balle rapide, faire le jeu, se taper une nana… sans cesse, sans fin. Amen.

L'église du baseball n'a pas connu d'assassinat, de Vietnam et encore moins de manifestations contre la guerre. Il n'y avait que le jeu.

À travers le regard de Neil Leifer, on s'extasie devant la beauté du baseball des années soixante et soixante-dix. La plus grande époque de ce sport. Les dieux hantent les photographies de Leifer : Mantle, Mays, Clemente, Koufax… Et ils nous ressemblent. Enfin… en mieux. Ce ne sont pas des hommes au corps artificiellement sculpté. Souvent d'ailleurs, ils ne sont pas très costauds : Henry Aaron était mince ; Willie Mays plutôt petit. Quant à Denny McLain… il me fait penser au petit gros avec son orgue Hammond B3 qui hante le salon de l'Holiday Inn. Pourtant, c'est aussi le dernier lanceur ayant gagné trente parties. C'était un sport différent à l'époque. C'était mieux. Il ne s'agit pas de nostalgie, mais d'un fait et, comme l'affirmait Casey Stengel : « Vous pouvez vérifier. ». Toutefois, si vous vérifiez, vous comprendrez que Casey a volé cette chute à James Thurber, l'humoriste américain. Et alors ? Après tout, on a le droit de voler au baseball.

On voyait des héros partout : McCovey, Mathews et Maury Wills. Même les immortels, tels Ted Williams et Stan Musial jouaient dans les années soixante.

Et les frères Robinson, Frank et Brooks, dans la même équipe, les Baltimore Orioles. En 1971, les Orioles comptent quatre gagnants de vingt parties. Oyez les prénoms de cette ère glorieuse : Gibby, Reggie, Pops, Maz et Yaz, Yogi. Inutile de citer leur nom. Thurman Munson, un vrai gars du Midwest, jouait pour les New York Yankees et Bill « Spaceman » Lee, un socialiste venu du sud de la Californie jouait avec les Boston Red Sox. Deux légendes, des compétiteurs féroces, dotés d'un ADN complètement différent, et pourtant liés par le baseball. Sans parler de la rivalité impitoyable entre leurs équipes.

À l'aube de cet âge d'or, le baseball se déplace vers l'ouest. Le derby entre quartiers de la Grosse Pomme « New York Giants contre Brooklyn Dodgers » traverse le pays et devient une rivalité entre deux villes plutôt décontractées et surtout distantes de plus de six cents kilomètres, San Francisco et Los Angeles. Huit ans plus tard le lanceur des Giants, Juan Marichal, donne un coup de batte sur la tête du receveur des Dodgers, Johnny Roseboro. Et voilà… la compétition a survécu à la migration transcontinentale. De toute façon, Californiens du sud et du nord ont été entraînés à se haïr afin que l'antagonisme survive et grandisse. Mais ce n'est plus qu'un rituel. À la fin du jeu, des séries ou de la saison, tout est pardonné.

Boston et New York, c'était tout de même autre chose. Une rivalité héréditaire. Impossible d'y échapper. C'était sacré, on avait presque l'impression d'appartenir à une secte… On en parlait à l'époque de l'Ancien Testament ou, du moins, depuis les années vingt quand le jeune Babe Ruth (« The Sultan of Swat », le sultan de la batte) avait été vendu par Boston à New York pour la somme de cent vingt-cinq mille dollars, créant au passage une petite industrie locale : « la malédiction du Bambino » (La malédiction en question voulait que Boston ne remportât plus jamais un titre après le départ du Bambino, Babe Ruth. Elle n'a pris fin qu'en 2004 !). Les Yankees et les Red Sox ne changeront jamais – c'est typique de la côte Est – et cette rivalité perdurera. Amen.

**Les années soixante et soixante-dix appartiennent à l'ère avant le grand capital,** lorsque les décisions importantes étaient prises par les managers et non par les ordinateurs. Une vraie carrière dans le baseball ressemble à celle d'Earl Weaver : joueur, entraîneur, manager, découvreur de talents, bref deux cent cinquante rencontres par an pendant quarante ans. Avec environ dix mille matchs au compteur, j'imagine qu'on peut commencer à se faire une opinion. Le manager Hank Bauer, un ancien Marine, et Al Lopez, ex-catcher de la ligue nationale : des types de terrain, des mecs qu'on n'a pas envie de contrarier. Un tempérament volcanique parfois, puis charmeur l'instant suivant, ce sont les derniers troufions devenus généraux. Et que faire de Casey Stengel, le vénéré manager new-yorkais, né à Kansas City, Missouri, et mort à Glendale en Californie ? Un visage marqué de mille rides. Des discours tonitruants, comme tirés de Lewis Carroll. Et pourtant – impossible d'ailleurs de savoir comment – il a su gérer avec une réelle délicatesse la collection d'ego

**Fielding practice, Spring Training, Miami Stadium, March, 1960**

**LEFT** Orioles pitching coach Luman Harris takes advantage of technology to get his troops in shape in spring training. One method for conditioning pitchers' legs is to hit fungos, high fly balls that make the pitchers sprint to catch them. Usually the coach hits fungos with a special bat, but this innovative machine did the job faster, more consistently, and with less strain.

**LINKS** Luman Harris, Wurftrainer der Orioles, macht sich im Frühjahrstraining moderne Technik zunutze. Eine Methode, die Beine der Pitcher in Form zu bringen, besteht darin, „fungos" zu schlagen, hohe Flugbälle, nach denen der Pitcher sprinten muss, wenn er sie fangen will. Normalerweise schlägt der Coach die „fungos" mit einem speziellen Schlagholz. Diese Maschine kann das aber besser und mit weniger Stress.

**CI-CONTRE** L'instructeur des lanceurs des Orioles, Luman Harris, tire avantage des nouvelles technologies afin de remettre en forme ses troupes lors de l'Entraînement de printemps. L'une des méthodes pour faire travailler les jambes des lanceurs consiste à frapper des «fungos» – des chandelles – qu'ils doivent attraper. Généralement, l'assistant-entraîneur utilise une batte spéciale, mais cette machine innovante remplit la même fonction plus vite, plus régulièrement et…sans effort.

démesurés qui hantaient les Yankees : de Mantle à Maris, de Ford à Berra en passant par Raschi. Observez le visage de Stengel. Il est le professeur, le clown, celui qui vous fait entrer dans le *Hall of Fame*, le Temple de la renommée. De tous les managers, Leo Durocher était le plus pittoresque d'une ligue majeure pourtant composée d'une fantastique galerie d'apaches – lorsque jouer sur une intuition semblait plus crédible que de taper des chiffres sur un ordinateur portable programmé selon les lois de la probabilité et les statistiques du baseball. Leo ? Les ordinateurs ? Il vous aurait dit : « À ton tour, fils. Ce type est petit bras en ce moment, alors fais-toi plaisir et défonce-moi cette balle. » (Traduction : « Le lanceur est épuisé. Tu peux réaliser un coup sûr. »)

Tout comme les joueurs, les managers sont des hommes qui se battent, jurent, picolent et, parfois, courent la gueuse. Un soir, en ligue mineure, je me suis faufilé dans l'hôtel après le couvre-feu et je suis tombé sur mon manager qui essayait de se taper une nana dans l'ascenseur. Lui et moi avons fait semblant de ne pas nous voir (j'ai pris l'escalier). Toutefois, ça m'a choqué. Autant que si j'avais vu mon père avec une autre femme. Pourtant, il ne s'agissait pas de mon géniteur. J'ignorais même si mon manager était marié et, en grimpant les marches sans faire de bruit, j'ai prié pour qu'il conclût : l'équipe était dans une mauvaise passe et je me disais qu'une bonne partie de jambes en l'air le détendrait. En plus, s'il couchait avec elle, il oublierait sans doute qu'il m'avait surpris pendant le couvre-feu.

Une règle non écrite et peu connue du baseball professionnel – quel que soit le niveau – stipule que les joueurs ne doivent pas boire dans les bars d'hôtel, domaine réservé au manager, aux entraîneurs et aux instructeurs. Serait-ce par crainte de voir se tisser des liens inavouables entre joueurs et managers ? Ou serait-ce, comme je l'ai toujours soupçonné, pour éviter qu'un joueur et un manager ne se retrouvent à draguer la même femme : un scénario à l'issue forcément tragique ?

Ces managers ont largement payé leur écot en passant leur vie sur la route, en épuisant femme, enfants et foie. Regardez-les, on dirait de vieux chefs indiens : notre version de Sitting Bull, Crazy Horse ou Geronimo. Hank Bauer, Ralph Houk, Charlie Grimm. Je leur laisse les bars d'hôtel. Je suis assez grand pour trouver un bistrot tout seul.

Le baseball n'est pas une métaphore de la vie ou de quoi que ce soit d'autre. En réalité, il ne ressemble en rien à la vie : ce qui fait en grande partie son charme. Jour après jour, il nous manque toujours du temps. Au baseball, non. Une horloge rythme notre existence de son tic-tac ; pas au baseball. Dans la vie, si on se plante, on n'a pas forcément de deuxième chance. Au baseball, on revient sur le marbre deux tours de batte plus tard. Et si on ne gagne pas le titre à la fin de la saison – comme toutes les équipes sauf une – pas de problème. « On attendra l'année prochaine. » On passera l'hiver, direction l'entraînement du printemps (Entraînements et matchs d'exhibition permettant à l'entraîneur de sélectionner son effectif final), une nouvelle floraison… un nouvel espoir.

**Le 20 juillet 1969 est marqué par deux événements.** Je joue deuxième base pour les Stockton Ports et j'ai une moyenne d'un sur quatre contre les Lodi Crushers, l'équipe réserve des Oakland Athletics. Par ailleurs, ce soir-là, la rencontre est interrompue pendant dix minutes pour diffuser le premier pas sur la lune de Neil Armstrong. On était sur le terrain, je m'en souviens encore, quand on a entendu sur la minuscule sono « Un petit pas pour l'homme… ». Je me suis tourné vers notre lanceur, Winston Presley de Compton, et je lui ai dit : « C'est quelque chose quand même, hein ? » Il s'est contenté de montrer la lune, pleine et brillante dans le ciel, et m'a répondu : « Impossible qu'il y ait un mec là-haut. C'est des conneries. » L'arbitre nous a appelés pour continuer le match. J'ai demandé à Winnie de « tenter de les éliminer, de lancer des balles basses », bref qu'on en finisse, pour pouvoir trouver un bar à Lodi avant la fermeture. On a continué de jouer.

Naturellement, même à cette époque – la fin des années soixante en Californie – Winston Presley aurait eu du mal à se faire servir dans un troquet de Lodi. Il était noir et les joueurs de Lodi vivaient dans l'immeuble de Stockton où nous logions, à une bonne trentaine de kilomètres. Ils ne se sentaient pas bien à Lodi. Pourtant, nous étions à moins d'une heure en voiture de San Francisco, l'épicentre de la contestation politique aux États-Unis. C'est également dans cette résidence que nous avons appris l'assassinat de Bobby Kennedy à la télévision quelques heures après un match. Deux semaines plus tôt, je l'avais vu prononcer un discours lors d'une réunion publique en plein air.

Ces juxtapositions représentaient la structure moléculaire de l'air que nous respirions dans les années soixante et soixante-dix. L'époque où Tiny Tim est devenu une star, pendant que John Coltrane suait sang et eau dans des restaurants miteux de Baltimore. L'époque de Norman Mailer et Jackie Susann, de Nixon et Warhol, d'Ali et Mary Poppins. Sur une chaîne Adam Clayton Powell, sur une autre *Laugh-In* et sur une troisième le massacre de My Lai. Stokely Carmichael, Betty Friedan, le général Westmoreland et Snoopy – pas étonnant que tout le monde ait abusé de drogues diverses et variées.

Sauf dans le baseball professionnel. En tout cas pas jusqu'à la fin de cet âge d'or, quand les drogues ont commencé à arriver sournoisement, d'abord comme distraction et ensuite pour améliorer les performances. Le speed, bien sûr. Mais ça ne compte pas. Qui peut reprocher à un joueur d'avoir gobé des amphés après dix-huit heures de car et deux parties le même jour à Little Rock par un après-midi d'août quand il fait plus de trente-cinq degrés ? Mais de la coke ? C'est un truc de junky. L'herbe ? C'est pour les hippies. Et les stéroïdes ? Ils n'existaient pas. Évidemment, tout cela allait changer, mais pas dans l'immédiat.

Les propriétaires dirigeaient d'une main de fer leurs équipes. Une fois la saison finie, les superstars travaillaient : qui comme vendeurs de voiture, qui comme baron pour fourguer des appareils ménagers sur les marchés. Mickey Mantle a gagné trente mille dollars l'année où il a remporté la Triple couronne de baseball. L'année suivante, son salaire a été doublé.

**Aujourd'hui, nous vivons à une époque où des batteurs à 0,280 signent des contrats de cinquante millions de dollars sur plusieurs années.** Willie Mays a gagné cent mille dollars en 1966. Le contrat de la star actuelle, Alex Rodriguez, lui garantit un quart de milliard sur dix ans. Si Mays et Mantle jouaient de nos jours, ils seraient propriétaires de leur équipe.

Tout a changé en 69, lorsque Curt Flood a refusé d'être vendu et est devenu la véritable Rosa Parks du baseball. Finalement grâce à un système de conciliation mis en place au début des années soixante-dix, la clause de réserve tant décriée (les sportifs jouaient leur vie durant pour leur employeur initial) a été abolie. Au bout de cinq ans dans une même équipe, un joueur pouvait se vendre au plus offrant. Les fans ont crié au scandale, mais une grande injustice venait de disparaître. Le baseball allait petit à petit se transformer. Pendant les années soixante-dix, le baseball a gardé sa pureté ; pourtant l'esprit des années soixante a tenté de s'infiltrer dans le jeu. On s'est mis à voir des barbes qui mangeaient les visages ou des casquettes perchées de façon précaire sur des coupes afro, pittoresques ou extravagantes. Des équipes bagarreuses, comme les excellents Oakland A du début des années soixante-dix, semblaient confirmer le chaos social et la volonté de changement n'affecteraient pas la qualité de jeu. Les joueurs d'Oakland se battaient sans cesse entre eux, mais une fois entrés sur le terrain, ils gagnaient trois World Series (Rencontres organisées entre les équipes championnes des deux ligues (« américaine » et « nationale ») de la ligue majeure (*Major League Baseball*) d'affilée. Leurs lanceurs s'appelaient Catfish, Blue Moon ou Vida Blue. Et Reggie et Rudy et Campy et…

Neil Leifer assistait aux World Series comme aux rencontres les plus banales du baseball quotidien. Banales certes, mais qui participent elles aussi de sa renommée. Les plus grands joueurs de tous les temps ont officié dans des stades remplis et devant des tribunes vides. On y joue tous les jours et contrairement au football américain professionnel, le baseball n'attend pas le dimanche après-midi, seize fois par an. Il n'existe pas en tant que produit télévisuel et ne bénéficie pas de la mode qui en résulte. Non, c'est tous les jours, cent soixante-deux fois par an, sans compter l'entraînement de printemps et les play-offs. Parfois, on dénombre cinquante mille spectateurs, parfois seulement mille cinq cents.

La quotidienneté un peu désinvolte de ce sport – à la fois le plus lent et le plus rapide de tous – fait qu'il n'est pas réglé par la montre. Pas de quart temps au baseball. Selon le mot célèbre de Yogi Berra : « Le match n'est pas fini tant qu'il n'est pas fini. » C'est le concept même du jeu : un espoir sans fin qui crée des moments de décontraction totale. Parce qu'il y a le temps : entre les manches, sous l'abri des joueurs ; du temps passé à discuter avec le joueur de première base adverse en revenant du but, au club-house, pendant les voyages en car ; l'attente en raison d'une averse interminable. Le jeu possède un rythme propre, des intervalles qui nécessitent d'être comblés et le langage devient leur ciment naturel.

**Charlie Finley surrounded by his players, September 1974**

**RIGHT** Oakland A's owner Finley (center) assembled a group of talented, combative players who took their disdain for Finley out on opposing teams, winning three straight championships from 1972 to 1974. The "mustache brigade" included Hall of Famers Rollie Fingers (top left), Reggie Jackson (center left), and Jim "Catfish" Hunter (bottom middle).

**RECHTS** Finley, der Besitzer der Oakland A's (Mitte) versammelte eine Gruppe talentierter und aggressiver Spieler, d, . die ihre Verachtung für Finley an den gegnerischen Mannschaften ausließen und von 1972 bis 1974 dreimal hintereinander Meister wurden. Zur „Schnurrbart-Brigade" gehörten die Hall-of-Fame-Stars Rollie Fingers (o. l.), Reggie Jackson (M. l.) und Jim „Catfish" Hunter (u. l.).

**À DROITE** Le propriétaire des Oakland A's (au centre) a constitué un groupe de joueurs talentueux et combatifs. Le mépris qu'ils manifestaient à son égard s'extériorisait contre les équipes adverses. Ils ont ainsi gagné trois championnats consécutifs entre 1972 et 1974. La «brigade des moustaches» comptait des membres du Temple de la renommée: Rollie Fingers (en haut, à gauche), Reggie Jackson (centre gauche) et Jim «Catfish» Hunter (au bas, au milieu).

**Il existe un jargon spécifique du baseball.** Lorsqu'on boit après une rencontre, on « hit the cocktail circuit » (tape le circuit des cocktails), raccourci plus tard en « circuit » (on tape le circuit) comme dans la phrase : «Tu tapes le circuit ce soir, parce que tu n'en as pas fait un seul depuis un mois ? »

L'art de lancer une balle vicieuse près de la tête du batteur afin de lui faire mordre la poussière – sans le toucher, évidemment – reste une tradition célèbre, quoique potentiellement mortelle, et se décline en plusieurs versions. On connaît le « knockdown pitch » (le lancer qui met K.-O.) pour d'évidentes raisons, mais il existe aussi le « brushback », comme si une balle rapide lancée à cent trente-cinq kilomètres à l'heure pouvait vraiment vous… décoiffer. Durant l'âge d'or, on se faisait poète et on évoquait d'une façon trompeuse la « chin music » (la musique du menton). Oui, c'est exactement ce que Bob Gibson et Don Crysdale me lançaient au menton – de la musique.

La balle rapide elle-même, « smoke » (fumée), « heat » (chaleur), « gas » (gaz) ou plus curieusement « cheese » (fromage) comme dans « Set him up outside with cheese on the black, waste a hook, then throw some gas in his kitchen ». La traduction littérale n'est pas nécessaire… mais pour les non-initiés, voilà tout de même ce que cette phrase signifie : « Balle rapide vers l'extérieur suivie d'une balle cassante hors de la zone de prises afin d'obliger le batteur à frapper sur un mauvais lancer et couronnée par une nouvelle balle rapide, cette fois à l'intérieur, juste sous les mains du batteur. »

Le home run (coup de circuit) se décline également. De l'évident « four bagger » (quatre bases) des premiers temps au postmoderne « yard » (terrain) : « He hit it out of the ball yard » (Il l'a frappée hors du terrain) est ainsi devenu « He went yard » (Il a fait le « terrain »). Durant l'âge d'or, dans les années soixante et soixante-dix, trois expressions sont devenues célèbres : « Dinger » qui donne par exemple « a lotta dingers in that bandbox » ce qui signifie qu'on assiste à beaucoup plus de coups de circuit dans un stade de petite dimension. « J'ai fait un 'homer', 'I rang the bell' (j'ai fait sonner la cloche), 'I took the sledgehammer at the carnival and drove the weight to the very top' (À la fête foraine, j'ai tapé avec la masse et j'ai fait monter le poids jusqu'en haut) » et, donc, le fameux « dinger ».

On évoque parfois le homer (home run) sous la forme « going downtown » (aller en ville). L'usage voudrait qu'on l'utilise dans une phrase telle que celle-ci : « The guy threw me a cock-high hangin' yellow hammer (bruant jaune) and I took him downtown » (littéralement : ce mec m'a balancé un petit oiseau jaune Le « yellow hammer » est donc une balle courbe). N'importe quel joueur, même âgé de huit ans, sait qu'une balle courbe médiocre à hauteur de taille deviendra sûrement un « dinger » pour l'adversaire. Et la délicieuse notion que le batteur « emmènerait en ville » le lanceur : ce n'est pas seulement la balle qui est frappée, mais l'ego du lanceur, ses statistiques, son amour-propre et peut-être sa carrière, et tous ces éléments sont déposés bien loin des gradins du stade… bref, en ville. Prends un bus et tire-toi de là, toi et ton lancer minable.

Enfin, le coup de circuit est parfois décrit par l'expression savoureuse quoique rurale de « long tater » (une grosse patate). S'agit-il d'une pomme de terre ou d'une patate douce ? Un « dinger » peut-il être doux comme la patate du même nom ? Raccourci en « tater », on le trouve dans ce genre de phrases : « He turned on that cheese and jacked him a tater » (« Il lui a retourné son 'fromage' bien enrobé dans une 'patate' ». C'est suffisamment clair, non ?

Les habitants de Brooklyn donnaient le surnom de *Bums* à leurs infortunés Dodgers. *Dem (Brooklyn) Bums*. Lorsque ceux-ci ont déménagé à Los Angeles en 1958, plus personne ne les a appelés ainsi. Les stars du cinéma sont arrivées et, un an plus tard, les Dodgers gagnaient les World Series, titre qu'ils avaient mis près d'un demi-siècle à conquérir quand ils jouaient encore à Brooklyn.

**« Dem Bums » ont un supporter passionné en la personne du jeune Neil Leifer,** élevé dans une cité du Lower East Side (le « vrai » Lower East Side) par un père employé des postes et grand admirateur de baseball. Neil vit à quelques stations de métro du Giants' Polo Ground, du Yankee Stadium et du Dodgers' Ebbets Field. Il assiste à toutes les rencontres, mais comprend très tôt que, pour devenir un vrai fan des Dodgers, il faut haïr les Yankees : c'est un engagement, comme dans une tribu. Son héros ? Le bloqueur des Dodgers, parce que Neil croit que Pee Wee Reese est le joueur le plus petit de la ligue… et lui pense être le gosse le plus petit du quartier. Le père de Neil soutient les Giants parce que leur joueur de troisième base, Sid Gordon, est juif. Le baseball leur apporte un nouveau sujet de dispute.

À douze ans, Neil Leifer s'inscrit au club photo du Henry Street Settlement, près de chez lui. Un émigré russe apprend la photographie aux gamins du quartier. Une fois par semaine, il confie un reflex bi-objectif DeJur et une pellicule à chaque enfant, et lui enjoint de revenir la semaine suivante pour développer les films. À treize ans, Neil se rend en métro aux rencontres et à quinze ans, il essaie de vendre ses photos ici ou là, généralement aux publications Dell Sports. Leifer se met à voir son sport bien-aimé à travers un objectif. Quant au monde, il voit désormais le baseball et ses héros comme jamais auparavant.

Très tôt dans sa carrière, Leifer a pris conscience d'un concept que, en connaissance de cause, j'ai illustré dans la plupart de mes films : l'essence du sport n'est pas de définir l'action… mais de cerner le temps qui s'écoule entre les actions. Il ne s'agit pas non plus de montrer les coups d'éclats, mais plutôt…le reste.

À dix-sept ans, Leifer s'efforce d'obtenir un laissez-passer de presse auprès de Dell Sports pour couvrir les World Series de 1960 entre les Yankees et les Pirates. *Sports Illustrated* accepte de développer les pellicules de Neil en échange d'un droit de regard. À l'époque, pas de tribune ou de places réservées aux photographes. On s'accroche à la tribune de presse, on partage cette vue d'ensemble avec les journalistes de la presse écrite et avec la principale caméra aérienne de télévision ; ou bien l'on s'accroupit sur le ciment dans une allée en espérant que personne ne vous balance une canette de bière parce que vous lui bouchez la vue. Neil commence à ressentir le besoin de s'acheter un boîtier professionnel, afin de pouvoir concurrencer les « huiles » de *Sports Illustrated*. Problème : ni lui ni son père ne possèdent quatre cent cinquante dollars. Neil va harceler son géniteur tant que celui-ci ne lui aura pas payé (en vingt-quatre mensualités) un Nikon F motorisé. Abraham Leifer n'avait jamais rien acheté à crédit et il éprouvait une grande fierté à ne pas avoir à rembourser de prêts ou des intérêts exorbitants. Neil lui promet qu'il lui rendra l'argent en livrant des sandwichs pour le Stage Deli de Midtown Manhattan. Son père rétorque en grommelant qu'il lui faudra des années pour solder ses comptes.

Les vétérans de la photographie chez *Sports Illustrated*, John Zimmerman, Hy Peskin, et Marvin Newman couvraient les Series pour ce magazine quand le jeune Leifer est arrivé et s'est mis à chercher une allée où il pourrait se tapir. Yogi court vers la deuxième base, Leifer le suit avec son nouvel appareil doté d'un téléobjectif et bingo ! Yogi est éliminé. Neil a l'angle parfait. *Sports Illustrated* achète la photo et la publie en couleur sur une page entière. Leifer empoche trois cents dollars. Deuxième manche : The Mick (Mickey Mantle) tape un coup de circuit, puis retourne vers l'abri des joueurs, Neil saisit cet instant. Image vendue, sortie le lendemain. Cent cinquante dollars supplémentaires. Il rembourse intégralement son père, démissionne de son boulot de livreur de sandwichs. Une carrière est née.

Les années suivantes, il va prendre certaines des photographies de boxe les plus connues au monde : à Lewiston dans le Maine, Muhammad Ali toise Sonny Liston ; il agite le poing, raille son adversaire déchu. C'est une image inoubliable du noble art parmi tant d'autres signées Leifer. Il place son appareil juste au-dessus du ring et, à l'aide d'un stroboscope, immortalise Cleveland Williams étalé de tout son long. Un instantané d'autant plus remarquable que l'on observe la photographie du crochet gauche d'Ali qui l'a expédié à terre, obtenue quelques millisecondes plus tôt par Leifer. Sa capacité d'anticipation et/ou sa chance ont toujours été insolentes.

Football américain, basket, Jeux olympiques, Leifer a imprégné notre conscience collective de plusieurs dizaines d'images.

« Mais le baseball reste le sport le plus difficile à photographier, » confesse Leifer. « Il faut attendre, attendre, attendre. » Voilà pourquoi, en revanche, il est facile d'écrire sur le baseball. Toute cette attente. Les supporters ont le temps de parler entre eux ; les joueurs aussi, même lorsqu'ils appartiennent à des équipes rivales. De quoi discutent-ils sur la première base ? Dans l'abri ? Sur le monticule ? J'ai essayé de répondre à cette question dans *Bull Durham* (*Duo à trois,* en version française). Mais franchement, toutes ces causeries ? Des assauts de courtoisie. Enfin jusqu'à la balle rapide qui fuse à cent quarante kilomètres à l'heure vers les poings du batteur ou la balle directe qui explose dans les pieds du joueur de troisième base.

> "Ninety feet between home plate and first base may be the closest man has ever come to perfection."
> —*Red Smith,* SPORTSWRITER, *THE NEW YORK TIMES*

« Quand il devient rapide, après l'attente, c'est vraiment le sport le plus rapide, ajoute Leifer, ce qui explique pourquoi il est si difficile de le photographier. Pendant une partie entière, j'ai braqué tous mes appareils sur le grand Brooks Robinson à la troisième base : personne n'y a envoyé de balle. »

« Même un combat de boxe navrant peut donner des images grandioses, ajoute-t-il, au contraire d'un excellent match de baseball dont il n'y a parfois rien à tirer. »

Ce qui nous ramène à ces instants entre les actions. Dans quel autre sport s'intéresse-t-on à ce qui se passe entre les moments forts ? Entre deux coups, au golf, rien ne bouge. Un temps mort au basket ? Un regroupement au football américain ? Au baseball tout se déroule entre les lignes, dans tous les sens du terme.

Observez attentivement « Match d'ouverture, 10 avril 1961 » au vieux Griffith Stadium à Washington. Le jeune JFK et le vice-président Lyndon Johnson, flanqués par Mike Mansfield et Everett Dirksen, sénateurs, et par le secrétaire à la Défense Robert McNamara regardent une grande chandelle. Y a-t-il quelque chose de moins intéressant dans le sport qu'une balle hors champ ? Pourtant, sur cette photographie, on voit les cinq hommes les plus puissants des États-Unis, avant l'escalade au Vietnam, avant la révolution sexuelle, Woodstock et Kent State, quand ce qui comptait – pour un instant du moins – se résumait à savoir si le tir allait être intercepté.

Autre image : Sinatra, Mia Farrow jeune et Leo Durocher, sémillants et décontractés, se détendent au Dodger Stadium. Des stars qui regardent des membres du Temple de la renommée. Combien d'avocats, d'attachés de presse, de représentants d'équipe et d'agents devraient être contactés de nos jours avant de pouvoir prendre une telle photo ? Et les joueurs ? Inutile d'essayer.

Pendant l'âge d'or, si un photographe souhaitait immortaliser une vedette du baseball, il lui suffisait de demander. « Si vous vouliez prendre une photo de Mantle, il fallait aller à l'entraînement des batteurs, attendre qu'il ait terminé et lui dire : 'Excusez-moi, M. Mantle, vous pouvez m'accorder cinq minutes ?' et, *plus souvent qu'à son tour*, il accédait à votre requête. » C'était oui ou non, simple ou expéditif, mais la tâche n'avait rien de complexe, ne nécessitait pas d'intervenir à plusieurs niveaux. Cette époque n'est plus. Aujourd'hui une séance photo avec Mantle requerrait des semaines de négociations avec toute une clique de représentants.

**Pourtant les photographies de ce livre nous ramènent à un baseball si ce n'est pur, du moins innocent.** Nous avons pardonné leurs cuites. Nous aimions leurs bagarres. Nous faisions semblant de ne pas être au courant de leurs coucheries. Ils portaient le nom de nos villes sur leur poitrine et, ainsi, nous *croyions* qu'ils s'intéressaient à nous… et si c'était une illusion, alors qu'on nous la rende. Les joueurs jouaient dur, ils signaient gratuitement des autographes, leur corps leur appartenait – et on les reconnaissait dans la rue.

Ils composaient notre équipe. Parfois leur vie durant. Mickey Mantle était un Yankee. Comme DiMaggio. Johnny Bench était un Red et Brooks Robinson un « O » (Orioles) pour toujours. Fidélité… sur le terrain de jeu.

Donc, ce n'est plus le cas de nos jours. Nous le savons tous. Et nous savons que des montagnes de fric ont transformé les joueurs en leur donnant ce sentiment d'impunité et ces privilèges qui les distinguent du commun des mortels. Ils ne nous regardent plus depuis un bail et ne veulent même plus nous parler. Je ne sais plus qui ils sont ou pour qui ils jouent. Difficile de mémoriser les noms dans une équipe, vu la valse des joueurs chaque année.

Ceux que Leifer photographiait, je les connaissais. Je voulais devenir comme eux. Neil captait bien plus que leur visage : leur façon de se détendre ou de se tenir dans le cercle d'attente, de s'accroupir dans le champ intérieur ou d'essayer de rattraper une chandelle dans l'allée (Zone double située entre le champ gauche et le centre, et entre le champ droit et le centre).

Chaque joueur avait un langage corporel propre, plus distinctif qu'une signature : on pouvait contrefaire l'autographe de Mantle, mais personne n'aurait pu imiter sa façon de trotter vers le champ centre ou de se retirer. Pas besoin d'un nombre de tirs, d'uniformes ou de programmes pour reconnaître les dieux. Or Leifer a trouvé la signature emblématique de chacun et l'a transcrite dans ses photos.

Par exemple, les gesticulations de Bob Gibson qui bondit du monticule, défie le batteur même après avoir lancé comme pour lui signifier « Non seulement je vais te battre, mais en plus je vais te dominer. »

La fluidité du mouvement de Don Drysdale, sa main droite qui vole, le dos tourné au marbre. Inimitable.

Le jeu de jambes acrobatique de Juan Marichal, aussi improbable qu'unique.

Henry Aaron, mince, détendu mais concentré, qui attend le lancer.

Roberto Clemente, toujours en mouvement, même dans ces photographies forcément figées. Déséquilibré, pas très orthodoxe, il est fluide, il est *l'athlète*.

Leifer a suivi le grand Clemente et a produit des volumes entiers de photos de ce membre distingué du Temple de la renommée. Le plus grand batteur droitier depuis la Deuxième Guerre mondiale -- sans doute possédait-il, en outre, le bras le plus puissant de l'histoire de ce sport. On le voit au charbon et avant d'y aller. Clemente au vestiaire, Clemente en train de se faire masser, Clemente se prélassant ou signant des autographes, Clemente dans sa chambre d'hôtel. Il a le visage d'un dieu grec, ce Portoricain qui joue pour les Pittsburgh Pirates. Jeune homme découvert par les Dodgers, il a été vendu en ligue mineure. Des années plus tard, il se porte volontaire pour aller distribuer de la nourriture et des fournitures médicales aux survivants du terrible tremblement de terre de Managua au Nicaragua. Son avion s'écrase au décollage. C'est la fin d'une fabuleuse carrière. Trois mille coups sûrs, une moyenne de 0,317 et une humanité qui a inspiré le Temple de la renommée : la période d'éligibilité, normalement de cinq ans, a été abolie

pour Clemente. Il est immédiatement intronisé. Et les jours de l'âge d'or sont comptés.

**Leifer a volé ces instants qui font une carrière.** On voit Mays rire, Aaron s'esclaffer ou Gil Hodges et son large sourire si typique. Et même Jimmy Piersall, pas très exubérant pourtant, le visage fendu d'une oreille à l'autre tandis qu'il frappe une balle à l'entraînement. Tout à coup, Leifer vous rappelle que ces hommes jouent à un jeu pratiqué par des gamins. Pendant un instant le rude Hank Bauer tire la langue, Billy Martin ressemble à un enfant de chœur et Reggie pousse Billy ; ils s'amusent comme deux gosses de huit ans. Et nous nous rappelons pourquoi nous aimons le baseball.

C'est une partie du récit de cet âge d'or, racontée par un photographe qui sait que les moments avant et après l'action condensent l'histoire.

Leifer nous offre toutes les facettes, tous les aspects du baseball. L'action et l'instant suspendu, paisible. Sans autofocus. Sans numérique. Quand le joueur de champ centre percute la clôture, Leifer le photographie avec un téléobjectif de six cents millimètres, réglé manuellement pendant le déroulement de l'action. Pas de deuxième chance. Il s'agit seulement du travail d'un grand photographe sportif sur le passe-temps national américain… lorsque c'était encore le cas.

Ces portraits de Neil Leifer nous unissent non seulement au baseball, mais aussi à nos pères, à notre enfance, à des souvenirs si intimes qu'ils ne peuvent être formulés autrement. Le premier gant, la première balle que l'on glisse dedans pour la façonner, la première partie organisée et le moment où votre copain de neuf ans vous lance une balle rapide à cinquante kilomètres à l'heure et l'humiliation ressentie quand vous revenez vers le banc en traînant votre batte, uniquement consolé par votre premier coup sûr, un roulant qui a rebondi une bonne vingtaine de fois et a échappé aux joueurs de champ intérieur. Et soudain, vous vous souvenez du premier instant où vos yeux se sont posés sur votre héros du baseball. Des années plus tard, plus âgé, vous comprenez que les dieux sont humains et qu'ils sont mortels… mais pas au baseball. Les photographies de Leifer nous autorisent pour un temps à mettre notre incrédulité entre parenthèses. Il voit le sport que nous ressentons et nous offre des images qui nous apaisent et nous émeuvent. Grâce à son œuvre, « on se sent comme chez soi ».

Est-ce que j'exagère ? Absolument pas. Ces photos me ramènent chez moi et je ne pense pas être le seul. Et c'est un don. Un don que même mon ami Neil n'apprécie pas à sa juste valeur.

# "It's a great day for a ball game; let's play two!"
## —Ernie Banks

### Elroy Face, pitcher, Pittsburgh Pirates

**PAGE 49** The great Pittsburgh relief pitcher from 1953 to 1968 perfected the "forkball" using an unusual grip with the ball held between two widely spaced fingers. A generation later, Bruce Sutter and others popularized the "splitter," a faster pitch using the same grip. Asked the difference between his forkball and Sutter's splitter, Face replied *"$3 million a year."*

**SEITE 49** Der großartige Pittsburgh-Pitcher, zwischen 1953 und 1968 immer wieder als Joker eingewechselt, entwickelte den „forkball", wobei er, höchst ungewöhnlich, den Ball mit zwei weit gespreizten Fingern hielt. Eine Generation später erfanden Bruce Sutter und andere den „splitter" – einen Wurf mit demselben Griff, aber schneller. Face auf die Frage nach dem Unterschied zwischen seinem Forkball und Sutters Splitter: *„Drei Millionen Dollar im Jahr."*

**PAGE 49** L'excellent lanceur de relève de Pittsburgh de 1953 à 1968 a perfectionné les lancers en « fronde » en saisissant la balle entre deux doigts très écartés. Une génération plus tard, Bruce Sutter, parmi d'autres, a popularisé une balle tombante plus rapide en employant la même prise. Lorsqu'on lui demandait la différence entre sa « fronde » et la balle rapide tombante de Sutter, Elroy Face répondait : *« Trois millions de dollars par an »*.

### A proud Podres, Los Angeles Dodgers vs. San Francisco Giants, Candlestick Park, August 21, 1965

**OPPOSITE** Head held high, Johnny Podres (#22) leads his teammates, catcher John Roseboro and second baseman Dick Tracewski to the clubhouse after two innings of strong work made him the winning pitcher in an extra-inning triumph over the Giants.

**GEGENÜBER** Mit erhobenem Kopf führt Johnny Podres (22) seine Teamkameraden Fänger John Roseboro und Second Baseman Dick Tracewski zum Clubhaus, nachdem er durch zwei starke Innings als Pitcher den Triumph in einem zusätzlichen Inning gegen die Giants gesichert hatte.

**PAGE CI-CONTRE** La tête haute, Johnny Podres (n° 22) guide ses coéquipiers John Roseboro et le deuxième base Dick Tracewski vers les vestiaires après deux manches d'un travail solide qui lui ont permis de devenir le lanceur vainqueur d'une manche supplémentaire gagnée triomphalement contre les Giants.

**Richardson turns two New York Yankees vs. Detroit Tigers, Yankee Stadium, May 14, 1961**

**OPPOSITE** Yankees second baseman Bobby Richardson backs away warily after throwing the ball to first base, watching the feet of Tigers runner Norm Cash bearing down on him.

**GEGENÜBER** Second Baseman Robby Richardson von den Yankees hat den Ball zum First Base geworfen, lässt sich jetzt aber vorsichtig fallen und beobachtet die näherkommenden Füße des Tigers-Runner Norm Cash.

**PAGE CI-CONTRE** Après avoir relayé la balle vers le premier but, le deuxième base des Yankees, Bobby Richard-son, bat en retraite avec méfiance en voyant s'approcher les pieds du coureur des Tigers, Norm Cash.

**Joe Torre, New York Mets vs. Milwaukee Braves, Polo Grounds, April 21, 1963**

**RIGHT** Young fans today who watch Joe Torre, the placid manager, don't realize what a top-flight player he was. A Braves catcher when he smacked this hit, moving in tandem with Mets catcher Choo-Choo Coleman, Torre played the infield for the last half of his 17-year career (1960–1977), winning a batting title and the Most Valuable Player award with the St. Louis Cardinals in 1971.

**RECHTS** Die jungen Fans, die heute Joe Torre beobachten, den gelassenen Trainer, ahnen nicht, was für ein hervorragender Spieler er war. Hier hat der sonst bei den Braves meist als Fänger eingesetzte Torre – mit Mets-Fänger Choo-Choo Coleman als Gegenspieler – gerade einen Ball geschlagen. In der zweiten Hälfte sei-ner 17-jährigen Kariere (1960–1977) spielte Torre im Innenfeld, gewann einen Titel als bester Schlagmann und wurde 1971 zum besten Spieler der St. Louis Cardinals gewählt.

**À DROITE** Aujourd'hui les jeunes fans de base-ball qui connaissent Joe Torre, le manager impassible, ignorent souvent son passé de joueur hors pair. Receveur des Braves à l'époque de ce coup sûr, on le voit bouger de conserve avec le receveur des Mets Choo-Choo Coleman. Torre a ensuite joué en champ intérieur lors de la seconde moitié de ses dix-sept ans de carrière (1960–1977). Il a remporté un titre à la batte et le prix de Most Valuable Player (meilleur joueur) avec les St. Louis Cardinals en 1971.

**Reggie Jackson, New York Yankees vs. Milwaukee Brewers, Yankee Stadium, April 7, 1977**

**BELOW** Reggie Jackson screws himself into the ground taking a home run cut during his Yankees debut. Signed as a free agent, Jackson declared himself *"the straw that stirs the drink,"* and for the next five seasons constantly entertained New Yorkers with his mighty swings, his mightier home run clouts, and his almighty ego.

**UNTEN** Reggie Jackson schraubt sich während seines ersten Spiels für die Yankees nach einem Homerun in den Boden. Als vertraglich ungebundener Spieler („free agent"), sah sich Jackson im Team als *„das Salz in der Suppe"* und unterhielt die New Yorker fortan fünf Spielzeiten lang mit seinen mächtigen Schwüngen, Homerun-Hits und seinem übermächtigen Ego.

**CI-DESSOUS** Reggie Jackson, vissé au sol, frappe un coup de circuit lors de ses débuts pour les Yankees. Engagé en joueur autonome, Jackson se définit lui-même comme *« la paille qui sert à remuer le cocktail »*. Pendant cinq saisons, il va ravir le public new-yorkais de ses préparations puissantes, de ses coups de circuit surpuissants et de son ego... tout-puissant.

**Play at second base, New York Yankees vs. Detroit Tigers, Yankee Stadium, June 23, 1973**

**OPPOSITE** When a runner tries to break up a double play, both he and the fielder are in danger. As Yankees second baseman Horace Clarke sails over Tigers runner Mickey Stanley to make the throw to first base, it's hard to tell whether Stanley is undercutting Clarke's legs or Clarke is kicking Stanley in the head. It's all part of the second-base ballet.

**GEGENÜBER** Wenn ein Läufer versucht, ein Double Play zu unterbinden, geraten beide in Gefahr – er selbst wie auch der Feldspieler. Während Horace Clarke, Second Baseman der Yankees, über Tigers-Läufer Mickey Stanley hinwegsegelt, um den Wurf zum ersten Base zu machen, ist schwer zu erkennen, ob Stanley Clarkes Beine untertunnelt oder ob Clarke Stanley an den Kopf tritt. Das alles gehört zum Ballett am Second Base.

**PAGE CI-CONTRE** Lorsqu'un coureur essaie d'enrayer un double jeu, le joueur de champ et lui-même sont en danger. Le deuxième base Horace Clarke passe au-dessus du coureur des Tigers, Mickey Stanley, afin de relayer en première base. Difficile de dire si Stanley cisaille les jambes de Clarke ou si Clarke donne un coup de pied à la tête de Stanley. Un grand classique du ballet qui se joue en deuxième base.

**"Minnie" Minoso, New York Yankees vs. Chicago White Sox, Yankee Stadium, circa 1960**

**PAGES 56-57** A forgotten star of the 1950s, Saturnino Orestes "Minnie" Minoso was one of the first Cuban players to excel in major league baseball. Smacking a base hit here with Yankees catcher Yogi Berra watching, Minoso combined speed, power, and a .298 lifetime average in a 15-year career.

**SEITEN 56-57** Saturnino Orestes „Minnie" Minoso, ein vergessener Star der 1950er, war einer der ersten exzellenten Kubaner im Major-League-Baseball. Hier schlägt er, beobachtet von Yankee-Fänger Yogi Berra, einen Base Hit, einen Schlag, der es ihm ermöglicht, das First Base zu erreichen. In seiner 15-jährigen Karriere kam Minoso, der Geschwindigkeit und Kraft zu paaren wusste, auf einen Durchschnitt von .298.

**PAGES 56-57** Vedette oubliée des années cinquante, Saturnino Orestes « Minnie » Minoso est l'un des premiers joueurs cubains à avoir excellé en ligue majeure. On le voit ici expédier un coup sûr sous l'œil attentif de Yogi Berra, le receveur des Yankees. Minoso, qui alliait vitesse et puissance, a atteint une moyenne de 0.298 durant ses quinze ans de carrière.

**New York Mets vs. Milwaukee Braves, Polo Grounds, April 21, 1963**

**OPPOSITE** Forget the popcorn, and never mind the camera. These young New York fans are only interested in catching the attention of one of their new favorites. In just their second year of existence, the Mets had captured the loyalty of what their manager, Casey Stengel, called *"the youth of America."*

**GEGENÜBER** Vergiss das Popcorn und die Fotografen. Diese jungen New Yorker Fans haben nichts anderes im Kopf, als ihre neuen Helden auf sich aufmerksam zu machen. Die Mets, obwohl erst im zweiten Jahr im Profi-Baseball dabei, hatten bereits die Herzen „*der Jugend Amerikas*" erobert, wie ihr Trainer Casey Stengel es formulierte.

**PAGE CI-CONTRE** Ils en oublient leur pop-corn et ne s'occupent même pas de l'appareil photo. Ces jeunes admirateurs new-yorkais sont concentrés sur un seul objectif: attirer l'attention de leurs nouveaux héros. Les Mets n'existent que depuis deux ans, mais ils ont réussi à susciter la loyauté de ce que leur manager, Casey Stengel, appelait «*la jeunesse américaine*».

**Early Wynn, pitcher, Chicago White Sox, circa 1960**

**BELOW** *"A pitcher has to look at the hitter as his mortal enemy,"* maintained Early Wynn, pitching here for the White Sox late in a career that included 300 major league wins. *"I have a right to knock down anybody holding a bat,"* said the man who relished his reputation as a mean, intimidating hurler.

**UNTEN** „*Ein Pitcher muss im Schlagmann seinen Todfeind sehen*", behauptete Early Wynn, der hier – gegen Ende einer Laufbahn mit 300 Major-League-Siegen – für die White Sox pitcht. „*Ich habe das Recht, jeden umzuwerfen, der ein Schlagholz in der Hand hält*", meinte der Mann, der seinen Ruf als aggressiver, Furcht erregender Werfer genoss.

**CI-DESSOUS** «*Le lanceur doit considérer le batteur comme un ennemi mortel*», affirmait Early Wynn qui, à la fin d'une carrière couronnée par trois cents victoires en ligue majeure, a lancé pour les White Sox. «*J'ai le droit d'assommer quiconque porte une batte*», fanfaronnait l'homme qui s'enorgueillissait d'une réputation de lanceur vicieux et intimidant.

**Manager Al Lopez, Chicago White Sox vs. Baltimore Orioles, Miami Stadium, early 1960s**

**BELOW AND OPPOSITE** We think of spring training as being for players, but for managers it's also a time to train umpires and to flex their own arguing muscles. Hall of Fame manager Al Lopez acts beleaguered as he lectures and harangues the men in blue, and it's still only March in Miami.

**UNTEN UND GEGENÜBER** Das Frühjahrstraining ist nicht nur für die Spieler da, auch die Trainer nutzen die Zeit, um Schiedsrichter auszubilden und ihre eigenen Argumentationskünste zu verbessern. Hall-of-Fame-Trainer Al Lopez wirkt geschafft, als er die Männer in Blau unterrichtet und beschimpft. Und dabei ist es erst März in Miami.

**CI-DESSOUS ET CI-CONTRE** On a tort de croire que l'entraînement de printemps ne concerne que les joueurs... En réalité, les managers s'y collent aussi en exerçant leur langue – souvent bien pendue – face aux arbitres. Al Lopez, manager et membre du Temple de la renommée, a l'air aux abois tandis qu'il sermonne et réprimande les hommes en bleu... et pourtant, on est seulement en mars.

## Ball players

**PAGES 78-83** Some great faces captured at "the Show": Joe Morgan (second base), Frank Robinson (right field), Jimmy Piersall (center field), Johnny Bench (catcher), Duke Snider (center field), Tony Perez (first base), Charlie Neal (second base), Whitey Ford (pitcher), Willie Tasby (center field), Jerry Lynch (left field), Al Smith (right field), Jackie Brandt (center field).

**SEITEN 78-83** Ein paar von den Großen während der „Show": Joe Morgan (Second Base), Frank Robinson (Right Field), Jimmy Piersall (Center Field), Johnny Bench (Fänger), Duke Snider (Center Field), Tony Perez (First Base), Charlie Neal (Second Base), Whitey Ford (Pitcher), Willie Tasby (Center Field), Jerry Lynch (Left Field), Al Smith (Right Field), Jackie Brandt (Center Field).

**PAGES 78-83** Ils ont tous fait partie du «Show»: Joe Morgan, (deuxième base), Frank Robinson, (champ droit), Jimmy Piersall (champ centre), Johnny Bench, (receveur), Duke Snider, (champ centre), Tony Perez, (première base), Charlie Neal (deuxième base), Whitey Ford, (lanceur), Willie Tasby (champ centre), Jerry Lynch (champ gauche), Al Smith (champ centre), Jackie Brandt (champ centre).

## Whitey Ford, New York Yankees vs. Pittsburgh Pirates, World Series Game Six, Forbes Field, October 12, 1960

**LEFT** Ford seems as perplexed as anybody following his second straight World Series shutout. Maybe he is simply astonished that his teammates made his job so easy, allowing him to win 10-0 and 12-0.

**LINKS** Ford fehlen nach seinem zweiten Shutout in der World Series einfach die Worte. Vielleicht ist er lediglich überrascht, dass seine Teamkameraden ihm das Leben erleichtert haben, sodass er mit 10:0 und 12:0 triumphieren konnte.

**A GAUCHE** Ford paraît lui aussi perplexe après ce deuxième blanchissage d'affilée dans les World Series. Ou peut-être est-il simplement abasourdi par le fait que ses coéquipiers lui ont rendu la tâche si facile en frappant, permettant ainsi de gagner 10-0 puis 12-0.

## Warren Spahn, late 1965

**OPPOSITE** Spahn, a perennial 20-game winner, won more games (363) than any other left-handed pitcher. After two decades with the Braves, he finished his career with the Giants as a grizzled 44-year-old veteran.

**GEGENÜBER** Spahn, der konstant 20 Siege pro Saison verzeichnete, gewann mehr Spiele (363) als jeder andere linkshändige Pitcher. Nach zwei Jahrzehnten für die Braves beendete er seine Laufbahn als angegrauter 44-Jähriger bei den Giants.

**PAGE CI-CONTRE** Warren Spahn, gagnant de vingt parties consécutives, est aussi le lanceur gaucher ayant remporté le plus de victoires (363). Avant deux décennies chez les Braves, de finir sa carrière avec les Giants, vétéran grisonnant de quarante-quatre ans.

**On the bench, Baltimore Orioles vs. Los Angeles Angels, Memorial Stadium, July 2, 1964**

**In the locker room, Los Angeles Dodgers, 1960s**

**OPPOSITE** Sitting on the bench provides only a sub-ground-level view of the field, so Orioles manager Hank Bauer perches on the back of the bench to get a better look at the action. Three seats past Bauer is Hall of Famer Robin Roberts, the only veteran on a staff of young starters just two years away from a World Series title.

**GEGENÜBER** Von der Bank im Spielergraben blickt man auf das Spielfeld wie aus einem Kellerfenster. Orioles-Trainer Hank Bauer hockt auf der Lehne der Bank, um die Action besser verfolgen zu können. Drei Plätze weiter rechts sitzt Hall-of-Fame-Star Robin Roberts, der einzige Veteran in einer Truppe junger Spieler, die zwei Jahre später die World Series gewinnen sollten.

**PAGE CI-CONTRE** S'asseoir sur le banc ne fournit qu'une vue partielle du terrain. Le manager des Orioles, Hank Bauer, préfère s'installer sur le dossier afin de bénéficier d'un meilleur angle sur l'action. À trois places de Bauer, le membre du Temple de la renommée, Robin Roberts, seul vétéran de cette équipe d'espoirs qui ne mettra que deux ans pour remporter les World Series.

**BELOW** Today's high-tech locker rooms feature big-screen televisions, booming stereos, and players absorbed in video games and investment portfolios. Things were simpler back in the 1960s, when this group of players gathered around flimsy stools for a pre-game rubber of bridge.

**UNTEN** Die Umkleideräume von heute sind Hightech pur mit Fernsehen auf Großleinwänden, dröhnenden Stereoanlagen und Spielern, die in Videospiele und Aktienportfolios versunken sind. In den 60ern war alles viel einfacher, wie diese Gruppe von Spielern zeigt, die auf wackeligen Stühlen vor dem Match eine Partie Bridge spielen.

**CI-DESSOUS** De nos jours, dans les vestiaires, on trouve des télévisions grand écran, des chaînes hi-fi et des joueurs absorbés par leurs jeux vidéo ou la gestion de leur portefeuille d'actions. C'était plus rustique dans les années soixante: assis sur des tabourets branlants, ces joueurs sont concentrés sur une partie de bridge.

## Pete Rose, Cincinnati Reds, May 1971

**LEFT** Brash and cocky, Pete Rose appears to be strutting while standing still. Thirty years old, in the prime of his career, the sparkplug known as "Charlie Hustle" couldn't help showing off his tight T-shirt touting the juggernaut Cincinnati Reds of the 1970s.

**LINKS** Pete Rose, keck und großspurig, scheint sogar, wenn er still steht, noch wie ein Pfau zu stolzieren. Mit 30 war „Charlie Hustle" auf dem Höhepunkt seiner Karriere und die Seele der Mannschaft. Er konnte gar nicht anders, als mit seinem eng anliegenden T-Shirt Reklame für die unaufhaltsamen Cincinnati Reds der 1970er zu machen.

**CI-CONTRE** Frimeur invétéré, Pete Rose semble se pavaner même quand il reste immobile. À trente ans, au début de sa carrière, « Charlie Hustle » (Charlie l'agité) ne peut s'empêcher de rouler des mécaniques dans son t-shirt moulant aux couleurs du mastodonte des années soixante-dix: les Cincinnati Reds.

## Close play at the plate, Cincinnati Reds vs. Pittsburgh Pirates, Three Rivers Stadium, May 26, 1971

**OPPOSITE** Three Hall of Famers debate a fine point of baseball law. Reds catcher Johnny Bench (middle) is incredulous at the ruling made by umpire Al Barlick, who calmly explains his reasoning. Reds manager Sparky Anderson, pushing Bench away so he won't be ejected, doesn't buy Barlick's argument either, but there's nothing he can do about it.

**GEGENÜBER** Drei Hall-of-Fame-Stars streiten über die Auslegung einer komplizierten Baseballregel. Reds-Fänger Johnny Bench (M.) ist fassungslos über eine Entscheidung von Schiedsrichter Al Barlick, der ruhig erklärt, warum er so entschieden hat. Reds-Trainer Sparky Anderson will das zwar auch nicht einsehen, weiß aber, dass er nichts gegen die Entscheidung tun kann, und schiebt Bench zur Seite, damit der nicht vom Platz gestellt wird.

**PAGE CI-CONTRE** Trois membres du Temple de la renommée débattent d'un point subtil des règles du baseball. On lit l'incrédulité sur le visage du receveur des Reds, Johnny Bench (au centre), tandis qu'il écoute les explications raisonnées de l'arbitre, Al Barlick. Le manager des Reds, Sparky Anderson, repousse Bench afin de lui éviter une exclusion, bien que lui non plus ne paraisse pas convaincu par l'argumentaire de Barlick.

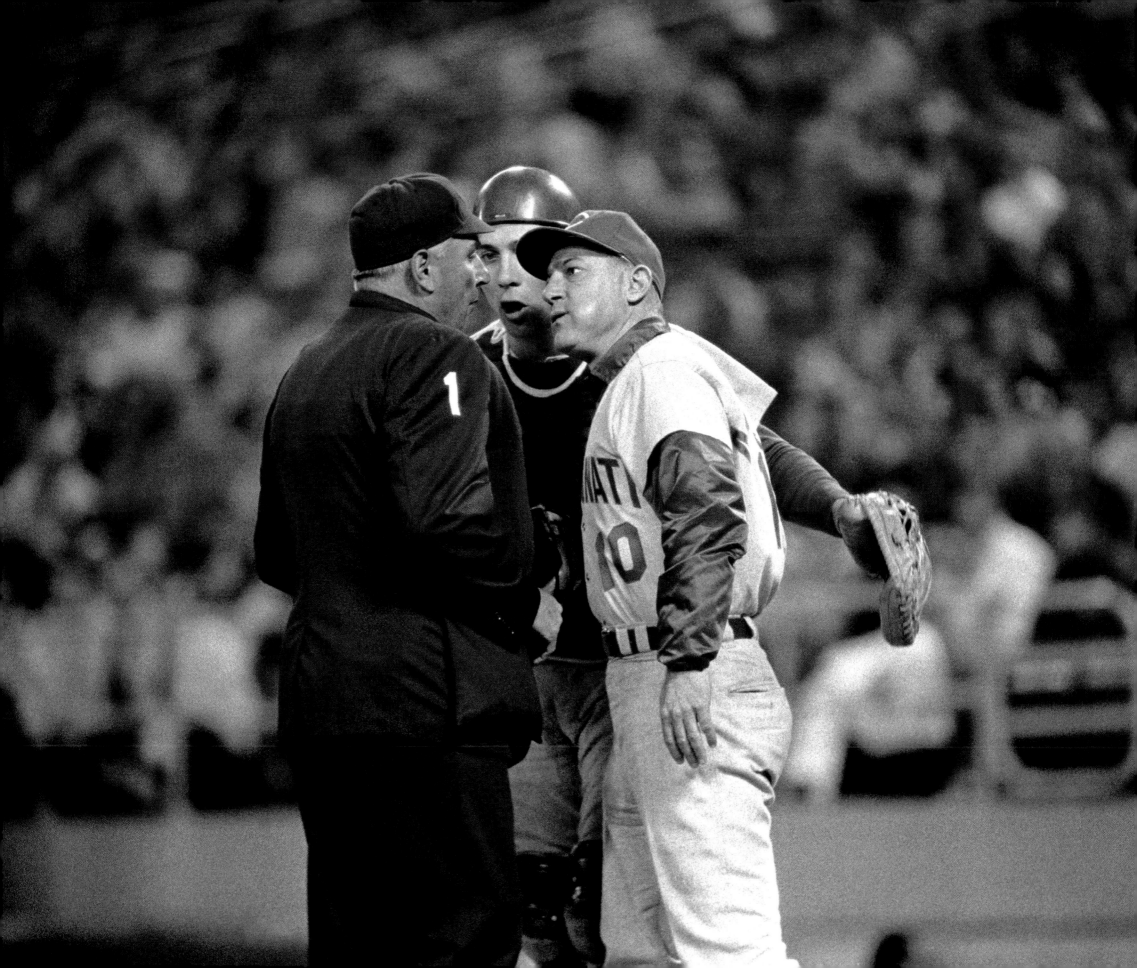

## Play at second, Pittsburgh Pirates vs. Philadelphia Phillies, Connie Mack Stadium, July 10, 1960

**OPPOSITE** Pirates shortstop Dick Groat toes second base as long as he can to catch the ball before jumping out of the way of the runner, Bobby Del Greco. These two players went in opposite directions in 1960. Groat won the MVP award with the champion Pirates, while Del Greco floundered in last place with the Phillies.

**GEGENÜBER** Um den Ball zu fangen, bleibt Pirates-Shortstop Dick Groat so lange wie möglich mit dem großen Zeh auf dem Second Base, bevor er Läufer Bobby Del Greco aus dem Weg springt. Für diese beiden Spieler nahm das Jahr 1960 einen gegensätzlichen Verlauf: Groat wurde als bester Spieler der Champions aus Pittsburgh ausgezeichnet, der gebürtige Del Greco dagegen landete mit den Phillies auf dem letzten Platz.

**PAGE CI-CONTRE** Dick Groat, bloqueur des Pirates, touche du pied la deuxième base aussi longtemps que possible pour attraper la balle avant de bondir hors de portée du coureur, Bobby Del Greco. En 1960, les deux joueurs ont connu des trajectoires opposées. Groat a remporté le titre de MVP (meilleur joueur) avec l'équipe championne, les Pirates, tandis que Del Greco suivait les Phillies dans leur chute à la dernière place du classement.

## Infielder Ernie Banks, Chicago Cubs

**RIGHT** A standout shortstop earlier in his career, the still-graceful Hall of Famer Banks glides from his first base position to field a ground ball. No Chicago player ever wore the cub on his sleeve more proudly. *"Let's play two!"* was his perennial cry, his sunny disposition matching his talent.

**RECHTS** Elegant wie eh und je, gleitet Hall-of-Fame-Star Banks – zu Beginn seiner Karriere ein Spitzen-Shortstop – von seiner Position am First Base, um einen aufspringenden Ball zu fangen. Keiner der Cubs trug das Clubabzeichen mit mehr Stolz als er. *„Lasst uns heute zwei Spiele machen!"*, war sein ständiger Schlachtruf. Sein sonniges Gemüt war ebenso bemerkenswert wie sein Talent.

**CI-CONTRE** Bloqueur exceptionnel au début de sa carrière, membre du Temple Ernie Banks, toujours gracieux, glisse depuis sa position en première base pour intercepter un roulant. Aucun joueur de Chicago n'a jamais porté avec plus de fierté les couleurs des Cubs. « Let's play two ! » (« Jouons deux parties ! », comme lors d'un programme double). Son naturel enjoué allait de pair avec un talent qui l'a rendu digne du Temple de la renommée.

## Denny McLain with Muhammad Ali, 1968

**BELOW** *"He might have the jumpingest fastball in the American League,"* wrote Alfred Wright in *Sports Illustrated* (September 23, 1968), *"but it is the incandescent flame of show biz that burns in Denny's heart."* In addition to appearances on the *Steve Allen Show* and the *Smothers Brothers Special*, McLain met fellow attention-hog Muhammad Ali during his whirlwind celebrity.

**UNTEN** „Er mag ja den sprunghaftesten Fastball in der American League werfen", schrieb Alfred Wright in *Sports Illustrated* (23. September 1968), „aber in Dennys Herzen brennt die leuchtende Flamme des Showbusiness." In seiner stürmischen Zeit des Ruhms trat McLain in der *Steve-Allen-Show* und im *Smothers Brothers Special* auf, außerdem begegnete er Muhammad Ali.

**CI-DESSOUS** « Il possède peut-être la balle la plus rapide de la Ligue américaine », écrivait Alfred Wright dans le *Sports Illustrated* du 23 septembre 1968, « mais c'est la flamme incandescente du show-biz qui brûle dans le cœur de Denny. » En plus de sa participation au *Steve Allen Show* et au *Smothers Brothers Special*, McLain, durant sa carrière tourbillonnante, a croisé une autre star des médias : Muhammad Ali.

## Another victory for Denny McLain, 1968

**OPPOSITE** Teammates congratulate Denny McLain after another of his 31 victories in 1968. *"Denny has always known what he can do with the baseball,"* said his pitching coach, Johnny Sain. *"Now he has learned the technique of doing it correctly. He knows a lot more about what he is doing than the 30,000 people in the ballpark think he does."*

**GEGENÜBER** Teamgefährten gratulieren Denny McLain nach einem seiner 31 Siege im Jahr 1968. *„Denny wusste schon immer, was man mit einem Baseball anstellen kann"*, meinte sein Wurftrainer Johnny Sain. *„Aber jetzt*

beherrscht er auch die Technik, es richtig zu machen. Er weiß verdammt gut, was er macht, besser jedenfalls, als die 30.000 im Stadion glauben."*

**PAGE CI-CONTRE** Ses coéquipiers félicitent Denny McLain après l'une de ses trente et une victoires de 1968. *« Denny a toujours eu conscience de ses capacités au base-ball »*, affirmait l'instructeur des lanceurs, Johnny Sain. *« Maintenant, il a appris la technique afin de procéder avec méthode. Il sait ce qu'il fait, contrairement à ce que croient les trente mille spectateurs du stade. »*

## New York Yankees vs. Baltimore Orioles, Memorial Stadium, August 14, 1964

**BELOW** Yogi Berra and Hank Bauer (#42) were teammates on seven championship Yankees teams between 1948 and 1959, but in the 1960s they found themselves opposing each other as managers. Here, they reminisce while exchanging lineup cards before a game, Berra piloting the Yankees and Bauer leading the Orioles.

**UNTEN** Yogi Berra und Hank Bauer (42) spielten zwischen 1948 und 1959 gemeinsam in sieben Meistermannschaften der Yankees. In den 1960ern standen sie sich dann als gegnerische

Trainer gegenüber: Berra bei den Yankees und Bauer bei den Orioles. Hier schwelgen sie, beim Austausch der Mannschaftsaufstellungen vor einem Spiel, in Erinnerungen.

**CI-DESSOUS** Yogi Berra et Hank Bauer (n° 42) sont coéquipiers lors de sept championnats des Yankees entre 1948 et 1959. Dans les années soixante, ils deviennent rivaux en tant que managers des Yankees (Berra) et des Orioles (Bauer). Avant la rencontre, ils échangent les feuilles d'ordre à la batte en évoquant de vieux souvenirs.

**Jimmy Piersall, New York Yankees vs. Cleveland Indians, Yankee Stadium, July 26, 1960**

**BELOW** Indians center fielder Jimmy Piersall's expression displays his fierce desire to excel even in batting practice. Referring to his youthful nervous breakdown, Piersall said, *"Probably the best thing that happened to me was going nuts. Nobody knew who I was until that happened."*

**UNTEN** Der Gesichtsausdruck des Indians-Mittelfeldspielers Jimmy Piersall spiegelt seine wilde Entschlossenheit, sogar im Schlagtraining zu glänzen. Über seinen Nervenzusammenbruch als Jugendlicher sagte er: *„Dass ich durchdrehte, war vermutlich das Beste, was mir passieren konnte. Denn vorher kannte mich niemand."*

**CI-DESSOUS** L'expression du joueur de champ centre des Indians, Jimmy Piersall, reflète son désir farouche d'exceller... même lors de l'entraînement à la batte. En évoquant la dépression nerveuse qui l'avait frappé durant sa jeunesse, Piersall affirmait : *« Je crois que la meilleure chose qui me soit arrivée, c'est de devenir cinglé. Avant, personne ne savait qui j'étais. »*

## New York Yankees Reggie Jackson and Billy Martin, 1977

**RIGHT** It was all fun and games for Jackson and manager Billy Martin early in 1977 after the free-agent slugger joined the Yankees. But by June, Jackson was tired of Martin getting all over his back, and when Martin removed him from a nationally televised game for not hustling in right field, the two had to be restrained from fighting in the dugout.

**RECHTS** Anfang 1977, als Jackson als „free agent" zu den Yankees kam, waren er und Trainer Billy Martin ein Herz und eine Seele. Aber spätestens im Juni hatte Jackson es satt, ständig von Martin genervt zu werden, und als Martin ihn während eines landesweit im Fernsehen übertragenen Spiels auswechselte, weil er sich im Right Field nicht ordentlich ins Zeug legte, gingen sich die beiden im Spielergraben beinahe an die Gurgel.

**A DROITE** Tout commence dans la joie et la bonne humeur lorsque le manager des Yankees, Billy Martin, recrute le frappeur Jackson sur le marché des joueurs autonomes. Toutefois, en juin, Jackson est fatigué d'avoir sans cesse son manager sur le dos. Martin le fait sortir du terrain lors de cette rencontre télévisée parce que, selon lui, Jackson ne trime pas assez sur le champ droit. Dans l'abri des joueurs, il faudra les empêcher de se battre.

## View from second base, Los Angeles Dodgers vs. Philadelphia Phillies, Dodger Stadium, April 25, 1965

**PAGES 110-111** A camera rigged under second base captures the fielder's foot about to step on the bag as Willie Davis of the Dodgers starts to slide, all under the gaze of the crowd packing the multi-tiered amphitheater of Dodger Stadium.

**SEITEN 110-111** Während die Menge von den voll besetzten Rängen des Dodger Stadium zuschaut, wie Willie Davis von den Dodgers seinen Rutsch zum Mal beginnt, erwischt eine unter dem zweiten Base montierte Kamera den Fuß des Feldspielers unmittelbar vor dem Betreten des Base.

**PAGES 110-111** Un appareil photo installé sur la deuxième base saisit le pied du joueur de champ qui s'apprête à toucher la base au moment où Willie Davis des Dodgers commence sa glissade. Le tout sous le regard de la foule entassée dans l'amphithéâtre à plusieurs étages du Dodger Stadium.

## Houston Astrodome, April 1966

**LEFT** The Astrodome was baseball's first domed stadium. The owners quickly discovered that grass wouldn't grow inside the stadium, so they replaced it with the "Astro Turf" seen in this view from the catwalk under the dome. Outfielders also had trouble seeing fly balls against the brightly painted ceiling, often missing them by 50 feet.

**LINKS** Der Astrodome war das erste Baseballstadion mit einem Kuppeldach. Die Betreiber merkten schon bald, dass im Stadion kein Gras wachsen wollte. Also verlegten sie stattdessen „Astro Turf", hier aufgenommen von einer Brücke unterhalb des Daches. Auch für die Outfielder gab es Probleme: Die hell gestrichene Decke blendete so sehr, dass sie hohe Bälle kaum erkannten und manchmal um 15 Meter verfehlten.

**À GAUCHE** L'Astrodome est le premier stade doté d'une coupole. Les propriétaires se sont vite rendu compte que la pelouse n'y pousserait pas; ils l'ont donc remplacée par l'«Astro-gazon» vu, sur cette photographie, depuis une passerelle sous le dôme. Les joueurs de champ extérieur avaient du mal à repérer les balles montantes qui se distinguaient à peine sur le plafond peint d'une couleur éclatante. Parfois, ils pouvaient les manquer d'une vingtaine de mètres.

## Fenway Park, 1976

**OPPOSITE** Tip O'Neill, Massachusetts congressman and speaker of the House, said that *"one of the reasons Sox fans are so good is the chumminess of the ballpark. It's like being in an English theater. You're right on top of the stage. It's intimate, it's homey, it's chummy. You feel as though you're in your own living room."*

**GEGENÜBER** Tip O'Neill, Kongressabgeordneter aus Massachusetts und Sprecher des Repräsentantenhauses, meinte: *„Einer der Gründe dafür, dass die Sox so gute Fans haben, ist die freundliche Atmosphäre des Stadions. Man kommt sich vor wie in einem englischen Theater. Man ist praktisch direkt auf der Bühne. Es ist gemütlich, heimelig, vertraut. Man meint, man sei in seinem eigenen Wohnzimmer."*

**PAGE CI-CONTRE** Tip O'Neill, représentant du Massachusetts au Congrès et président de la Chambre des représentants, déclarait: *«Les Sox sont des spectateurs fantastiques. Savez-vous pourquoi? En raison de la convivialité de notre stade. On y est comme dans un petit théâtre anglais, juste à côté de la scène. C'est intime, vivant, presque familial. On a l'impression d'être chez soi, dans son séjour.»*

## Rain delay, Los Angeles Dodgers vs. Philadelphia Phillies

**OPPOSITE** When rain interrupts a game, the adults scurry for cover. But for kids, a downpour affords an opportunity to do three of their favorite things: get near a major league dugout where they might see a player, romp in the rain, and clown in front of a camera.

**GEGENÜBER** Bei einer Regen-Unterbrechung suchen die Erwachsenen so schnell wie möglich Schutz. Die Jugendlichen dagegen nutzen die Gelegenheit für drei ihrer Lieblingsbeschäftigungen: Sie versuchen, in die Nähe eines Spielergrabens zu kommen, um vielleicht einen Spieler zu sehen, sie tollen im Regen und albern vor den Kameras herum.

**PAGE CI-CONTRE** Lorsque la pluie interrompt une partie, les adultes courent s'abriter. Mais pour les enfants, une bonne averse permet surtout de pratiquer trois de leurs activités préférées: s'approcher de l'abri d'une ligue majeure afin de voir une vedette, jouer sous l'eau et faire les clowns devant l'appareil photo.

## Tom Yawkey, owner, Boston Red Sox, Fenway Park, July 1975

**RIGHT** The landscape of Fenway Park is reflected in the glasses of Red Sox owner Tom Yawkey. After buying the team in 1933, Yawkey spent millions of dollars trying to buy a championship, only to fall just short. Growing old with his team, he found disappointment again in 1975 when the Red Sox lost the World Series in seven games. He died the next year.

**RECHTS** In der Brille des Red-Sox-Besitzers Tom Yawkey spiegelt sich der Fenway Park. Nachdem Yawkey das Team 1933 gekauft hatte, versuchte er mit Millionen von Dollar, auch eine Meisterschaft zu erkaufen – vergebens. Er wurde gemeinsam mit seinem Team alt und erlebte 1975 eine weitere Enttäuschung, als die Red Sox die World Series nach sieben Spielen verloren. Ein Jahr später verstarb er.

**À DROITE** Le Fenway Park se reflète dans les lunettes du propriétaire des Red Sox, Tom Yawkey. Après avoir acheté l'équipe en 1933, Yawkey a dépensé des millions de dollars pour essayer de gagner un titre... qu'il n'a jamais remporté. Il vieillit avec son équipe. En 1975, nouvelle déception: les Red Sox perdent les World Series en sept matchs. Yawkey décède l'année suivante.

## Team photo, Baltimore Orioles, 1965

**PAGES 116-117** Orioles general manager Lee MacPhail, like his father Larry a Hall of Fame electee as an executive, is flanked by manager Hank Bauer (to his left, #42) and pitching coach Harry Brecheen in this team photo taken the year before the Orioles shocked the baseball world with their upset World Series victory over the Dodgers.

**SEITEN 116-117** Lee MacPhail, General Manager der Orioles und wie sein Vater Larry als leitender Angestellter in die Hall of Fame gewählt, sitzt hier zwischen Trainer Hank Bauer (l., 42) und Wurftrainer Harry Brecheen auf einem Mannschaftsfoto, das ein Jahr vor dem Sensationssieg der Orioles in der World Series gegen die Dodgers aufgenommen wurde.

**PAGES 116-117** Le manager général des Orioles, Lee MacPhail, membre du Temple de la renommée en tant que cadre de l'équipe (comme son père, Larry, avant lui) est flanqué du manager Hank Bauer (à sa gauche, n° 42) et de l'instructeur des lanceurs Harry Brecheen, sur cette photo prise l'année précédant la victoire déroutante des Orioles sur les Dodgers en World Series. Une victoire qui a bouleversé le monde du base-ball.

## New York Yankees vs. Detroit Tigers, Yankee Stadium, June 24, 1973

**BELOW** George Steinbrenner, new owner of the Yankees, sits with his wife, Joan, in box seats behind the dugout, surrounded by fans. *"I won't be active in the day-to-day operations of the club at all,"* he declared when he purchased baseball's premium franchise. Thirty-five years later, presiding from an enclosed suite above the action, he remains the most meddlesome owner in baseball history.

**UNTEN** Umgeben von Fans sitzt George Steinbrenner, der neue Eigentümer der Yankees, mit Ehefrau Joan in einer Loge hinter dem Spielergraben. *„Ins Alltagsgeschäft des Clubs werde ich mich keinesfalls einmischen"*, erklärte er, als er das Aushängeschild des Baseballs kaufte. 35 Jahre später, inzwischen in einer abgeschlossenen separaten Suite oberhalb des Geschehens, mischt er sich unverändert so sehr in alles Mögliche ein wie kein anderer Eigentümer in der Geschichte des Baseballs.

**CI-DESSOUS** George Steinbrenner, le nouveau propriétaire des Yankees, est assis en compagnie de sa femme Joan derrière l'abri des joueurs, dans le public. « *Je n'interviendrai pas dans les affaires quotidiennes du club* », a-t-il déclaré en achetant cette équipe exceptionnelle. Trente-cinq ans plus tard, il préside depuis une suite fermée située juste au dessus de l'action. De toute l'histoire du base-ball, il demeure sans aucun doute le propriétaire qui est le plus intervenu dans la gestion de sa franchise.

## St. Louis Cardinals, 1967

**RIGHT** The colorful 1967 champions featured four Hall of Famers—manager Red Schoendienst (in uniform), Bob Gibson, Lou Brock, and Orlando Cepeda—along with significant figures Roger Maris, Tim McCarver, and Curt Flood. Even the last man in the lineup, weak-hitting shortstop Dal Maxvill, made a name for himself later as a general manager.

**RECHTS** Zur schillernden Meistermannschaft von 1967 zählten vier Stars aus der Hall of Fame: Trainer Red Schoendienst (im Trikot), Bob Gibson, Lou Brock und Orlando Cepeda – sowie so bedeutende Leute wie Roger Maris, Tim McCarver und Curt Flood. Sogar der Letzte in der Schlagreihenfolge, der schwach schlagende Shortstop Dal Maxvill, machte sich später noch einen Namen als General Manager

**À DROITE** Champions en 1967, les Cardinals – équipe haute en couleur s'il en est –alignent quatre membres du Temple de la renommée (le manager Red Schoendienst, en uniforme, Bob Gibson, Lou Brock et Orlando Cepeda) parmi d'autres joueurs célèbres comme Roger Maris, Tim McCarver et Curt Flood. Même le dernier homme sur la feuille d'ordre, le bloqueur Dal Maxvill, pourtant faible à la batte, s'est plus tard fait un nom en tant que manager général.

## Houston Astros vs. New York Mets, Astrodome, May 24, 1966

**BELOW** Indoor baseball brought some aberrant playing conditions that weren't covered in the basic rules. During this pre-game meeting, umpire Paul Pryor points out to Mets manager Wes Westrum what will happen if a fly ball strikes one of the speakers or other structures hanging from the ceiling of the Astrodome.

**UNTEN** Baseball in der Halle führte zu ungewöhnlichen Situationen, die in den Regeln nicht vorgesehen sind. Vor dem Spiel erklärt Schiedsrichter Paul Pryor dem Trainer der Mets, Wes Westrum, was passiert, wenn ein hoher Ball einen der Lautsprecher oder andere von der Decke des Astrodomes herabhängende Teile trifft.

**CI-DESSOUS** Le base-ball dans un stade couvert provoque des situations de jeu absurdes et qui ne sont pas prévues par le règlement. Au cours de cette réunion d'avant match, l'arbitre Paul Pryor explique au manager des Mets, Wes Westrum, la procédure si une chandelle percute un haut-parleur ou un autre élément suspendu au plafond de l'Astrodome.

### Beneath the grandstand, New York Yankees vs. Cleveland Indians, Yankee Stadium, August 26, 1960

**RIGHT** This view from a walkway underneath the grandstand beautifully frames the action at home plate while fans in the lower boxes and at an upstairs railing watch the first-place Yankees sweep a doubleheader from the Indians en route to another American League pennant.

**RECHTS** Dieser Blick aus einem Gang unterhalb der Haupttribüne rahmt sehr schön das Geschehen am Schlagmal ein. Die Zuschauer in den unteren Logen und am oberen Geländer wurden Zeugen, wie die Yankees auf dem Weg zu einem weiteren Meistertitel der American League einen Doubleheader gegen die Indians gewannen.

**À DROITE** Cette vue, prise d'une passerelle sous les tribunes, cadre magnifiquement l'action autour du marbre au moment où les spectateurs des gradins inférieurs et ceux appuyés contre la balustrade observent les Yankees, en tête du classement, qui balaient les Indians lors d'un programme double, en route une nouvelle fois vers le titre de la Ligue américaine.

### Perennial pennant winners, New York Yankees vs. Baltimore Orioles, Memorial Stadium, September 20, 1961

**PAGES 122-123** The Yankees are all smiles after beating the Orioles 4-2 to clinch their 12th American League pennant in 15 years. The celebrants include (left to right): Roger Maris, who hit his 59th home run in this game; Johnny Blanchard; Elston Howard; first-year manager Ralph Houk; and winning pitcher Ralph Terry. They went on to win the World Series.

**SEITEN 122-123** Die Yankees haben gut lachen nach ihrem 4:2-Sieg gegen die Orioles, der ihnen den 12. Meistertitel der American League in 15 Jahren sicherte. Unter den Feiernden (v. l. n. r.): Roger Marris, der in diesem Spiel seinen 59. Homerun schlug, Johnny Blanchard, Elston Howard, Ralph Houk in seinem ersten Jahr als Trainer und Pitcher Ralph Terry. Als Nächstes gewannen sie die World Series.

**PAGES 122-123** Les Yankees, tout sourire après avoir battu les Orioles 4-2, accrochent un douzième titre de la Ligue américaine en quinze ans. On reconnaît (de gauche à droite): Roger Maris (qui a frappé son 59e coup de circuit durant cette partie); Johnny Blanchard; Elston Howard; Ralph Houk (pour sa première année en tant que manager); et le lanceur gagnant Ralph Terry. L'équipe poursuivra sur sa lancée en gagnant les World Series.

"I think that both baseball and the country will endure."
— *President John F. Kennedy*

**Washington Senators vs. Chicago White Sox, Griffith Stadium, April 10, 1961**

**OPPOSITE** On the 81st day of his presidency, John F. Kennedy helped inaugurate the second incarnation of the Washington Senators by continuing the long-standing presidential tradition of throwing out the ceremonial first pitch of the season. Accompanied by Vice President Lyndon Johnson, Kennedy watched the home team lose, also a Senators tradition.

**GEGENÜBER** Am 81. Tag seiner Präsidentschaft, beim zweiten Auftritt eines Teams der Washington Senators in der Major League, setzte John F. Kennedy eine alte Tradition fort: Der Präsident warf den zeremoniellen ersten Ball der Saison. Begleitet von Vizepräsident Lyndon Johnson sah Kennedy dann zu, wie die Senators das Spiel verloren – was ebenfalls Tradition hatte.

**PAGE CI-CONTRE** Le 81e jour de sa présidence, Kennedy participe au match saluant la nouvelle incarnation de l'équipe des Washington Senators. En lançant la première balle de la saison, il s'inscrit dans une longue tradition présidentielle. Accompagné par le vice-président Lyndon Johnson, Kennedy assiste à la défaite des Senators à domicile... une autre tradition bien ancrée.

"Sometimes I sit in my den at home and read stories about myself. Kids used to…mail them to me. I'll go in there and read them, and you know what? They might as well be about Musial and DiMaggio, it's like reading about somebody else."

—*Mickey Mantle*

### Mickey Mantle, New York Yankees vs. Washington Senators, April 30, 1961

**PAGE 127** Mantle grimaces as he reaches first base just in time to avoid a double play. Thirty years old, his legs already decimated by injuries, he was in agony every time he had to run hard. Star center fielder for the Yankees from 1951 to 1968, Mantle won the American League Triple Crown in 1956 and holds the career record with 18 World Series home runs.

**SEITE 127** Mantle verzerrt das Gesicht, als er gerade noch rechtzeitig das erste Base erreicht, um ein Double Play der Senators zu verhindern. Bei jedem schnellen Lauf litt der 30-jährige Mantle entsetzliche Schmerzen, denn seine Beine waren durch viele Verletzungen schwer geschädigt. Mantle war von 1951 bis 1968 der Star im Center Field der Yankees. Er gewann 1956 die Triple Crown der American League und hält mit 18 Homeruns in der World Series den Laufbahn-Rekord.

**PAGE 127** Mantle grimace de douleur en touchant la première base juste à temps pour éviter un double jeu. À trente ans, Mantle souffrait de plusieurs blessures aux jambes et endurait le martyr dès qu'il devait courir un peu vite. Le champ centre vedette des Yankees entre 1951 et 1968 a gagné la Triple couronne de la Ligue américaine en 1956 et, avec dix-huit « home runs », détient le record de coups de circuit frappés en World Series.

### The great #7, New York Yankees vs. Baltimore Orioles, Yankee Stadium

**OPPOSITE** With the growth of television, the "Game of the Week," and his annual World Series feats in the 1950s, Mantle came to represent baseball to a generation of fans nationwide.

**GEGENÜBER** Durch den Siegeszug des Fernsehens, das „Spiel der Woche" und seine meisterhaften World-Series-Auftritte in den 1950er-Jahren wurde Mantle landesweit für eine ganze Generation zur Symbolfigur des Baseball.

**PAGE CI-CONTRE** Grâce à la télévision, notamment l'émission « Le match de la semaine », et grâce à ses exploits annuels lors des World Series, Mickey Mantle est devenu l'incarnation du base-ball pour une génération entière de fans dans tout le pays.

## "The Mick" runs to first

**OPPOSITE** *"Hitting the ball was easy. Running around the bases was the tough part."* Mantle suffered so many devastating leg injuries that for the last half of his career, he had to be bandaged from his hips to his feet before every game just so he could play.

**GEGENÜBER** *„Den Ball zu treffen war einfach. Das Schlimme war der Lauf von Base zu Base."* Mantle erlitt so viele schlimme schwere Beinverletzungen, dass er in der zweiten Hälfte seiner Laufbahn vor jedem Spiel von der Hüfte bis zu den Füßen bandagiert werden musste, um überhaupt antreten zu können.

**PAGE CI-CONTRE** *« Frapper la balle, c'est facile. Le plus dur, c'est de faire le tour des bases. »* Mantle souffrait de blessures multiples aux jambes. Durant la deuxième moitié de sa carrière, s'il voulait pouvoir jouer, il devait se bander de la taille aux pieds avant chaque rencontre.

## Switch-hitter Mickey Mantle

**BELOW** The greatest switch-hitter ever, Mantle scared pitchers from both sides of the plate. He hit home runs more often as a left-handed batter, but seemed to hit them farther right-handed. When he retired in 1968, his 536 homers trailed only Babe Ruth and Willie Mays on the all-time list.

**UNTEN** Mantle, der bedeutendste beidhändige Schlagmann aller Zeiten, jagte den Pitchern Angst ein, egal ob er mit links oder mit rechts schlug. Mit links schlug er mehr Homeruns, mit rechts schienen die Bälle weiter zu fliegen. Bei seinem Rücktritt 1968 hatte er es auf 536 Homeruns gebracht, übertroffen nur von Babe Ruth und Willie Mays.

**CI-DESSOUS** Le plus grand des frappeurs ambidextres, Mantle s'est imposé face aux lanceurs des deux côtés du marbre. Il a réussi davantage de coups de circuit à gauche, mais paraissait plus puissant du côté droit. Lorsqu'il se retire en 1968, avec ses 536 coups de circuit, seuls Babe Ruth et Willie Mays le surpassent.

**Mantle at work, New York Yankees vs. San Francisco Giants in World Series Game Four, Yankee Stadium, October 8, 1962**

**PAGES 132-133** This is the swing a generation of fans and fellow players idolized—Mickey Mantle's exquisitely balanced explosion of raw power, his left knee bent for extra leverage. Catcher Tom Haller and umpire Jim Honochick barely have time to flinch as the ball rockets off the bat.

**SEITEN 132-133** Dies ist der Schlag, von dem eine Generation von Fans und Mitspielern schwärmte – Mickey Mantles großartig ausbalancierte Explosion roher Kraft, das linke Knie gebeugt, um die Hebelwirkung zu vergrößern. Fänger Tom Haller und Schiedsrichter Jim Honochick stockt der Atem, als der Schläger den Ball wie eine Rakete beschleunigt.

**PAGES 132-133** Le mouvement qu'une génération de fans et de joueurs de base-ball a idolâtré: l'explosion de puissance brute de Mickey Mantle, pourtant délicatement équilibrée. On remarque le genou gauche plié pour obtenir un gain de force. Le receveur Tom Haller et l'arbitre Jim Honochick ont à peine le temps de sourciller que la balle fuse déjà, renvoyée par la batte.

**The Bronx Bombers, New York Yankees vs. Pittsburgh Pirates, Forbes Field, October 1960**

**BELOW** Roger Maris, Mickey Mantle, and Clete Boyer flaunt their championship expectations following one of their three romps in the 1960 World Series. Their Yankees embarrassed the Pirates by scores of 16-3, 10-0, and 12-0. But there's a tinge of doubt in the trio's bravado. Somehow, the Pirates won the other four games, all close contests, to take the title.

**UNTEN** Roger Maris, Mickey Mantle und Clete Boyer fühlen sich nach einem ihrer drei leichten Siege in der World Series 1960 schon als Champions. Mit 16:3, 10:0 und 12:0 hatten ihre Yankees den Pirates drei peinliche Niederlagen bereitet. Aber bei aller Siegesgewissheit des Trios blieb doch ein Hauch von Zweifel. Und tatsächlich gewannen die Pirates die restlichen vier Spiele – zwar nur sehr knapp, aber sie holten den Titel.

**CI-DESSOUS** Roger Maris, Mickey Mantle et Clete Boyer affichent clairement leur objectif – gagner le titre – après trois victoires faciles dans les World Series de 1960. Les Yankees ont en effet humilié les Pirates sur des résultats de 16-3, 10-0 et 12-0. Toutefois, on perçoit le doute qui pointe sous les fanfaronnades du trio. Surprise: les Pirates remportent de vive lutte les quatre dernières parties et empochent le titre.

**Batting practice, New York Yankees vs. Cleveland Indians, Yankee Stadium, July 26, 1960**

**OPPOSITE** Half the starting lineup relaxes around the batting cage: Mantle (#7), Maris (#9), Tony Kubek (#10), and Moose Skowron (#14). Possessing the magical ability to elevate their performance when it mattered most, the 1960 Yankees were tied for the American League lead with 15 games left, and won all 15 to cruise to the first of five straight pennants.

**GEGENÜBER** Die Hälfte der Startbesetzung entspannt sich am Schlaggitter: Mantle (7), Maris (9), Tony Kubek (10) und Moose Skowron (14). 1960 lagen die Yankees 15 Spiele vor Ende der Serie gleichauf an der Spitze der American League. Dank ihrer Fähigkeit, immer dann zur Hochform aufzulaufen, wenn es besonders wichtig war, gewannen sie die restlichen 15 Spiele und sicherten sich den ersten von fünf aufeinanderfolgenden Titeln.

**PAGE CI-CONTRE** La moitié de l'effectif de départ se détend près du tunnel de frappe: Mantle (n° 7), Roger Maris (n° 9), Tony Kubek (n° 10) et Moose Skowron (n° 14). Les Yankees des années soixante, qui possédaient cette capacité magique d'élever leur niveau de jeu lorsqu'il le fallait, se partagent la première place de la Ligue américaine. Il reste quinze parties. Ils les remporteront toutes, ainsi que le titre, le premier d'une série de cinq consécutifs.

## "Hammerin' Hank," Milwaukee Braves vs. New York Mets, Polo Grounds, April 19, 1963

**LEFT AND OPPOSITE** Aaron built his success on the quickest wrists in baseball. Facing Roger Craig of the Mets, who had a shutout going in the eighth inning, Aaron waits on the ball, then uses a compact, fast swing that produces a short follow-through compared to those of fellow sluggers Willie Mays and Mickey Mantle. Aaron and Craig turn to gaze at the blast that spells the end of Craig's shutout.

**LINKS UND GEGENÜBER** Aaron verdankt seinen Erfolg den schnellsten Handgelenken im Baseball. Ihm gegenüber Roger Craig von den Mets, der im achten Inning bislang keinen Punkt zugelassen hat. Aaron erwartet den Ball, nimmt dann kurz und schnell Schwung und produziert einen kurzen, überaus scharfen Ball. Aaron und Craig starren dem wuchtigen Schlag hinterher, der das Ende von Craigs Shutout bedeutet.

**À GAUCHE ET PAGE CI-CONTRE** Aaron a construit son succès sur ses poignets, les plus rapides du base-ball. Roger Craig des Mets a éliminé tous les batteurs dans cette huitième manche. Aaron attend la balle et frappe un coup rapide et dense qu'il accompagne peu par rapport à d'autres cogneurs comme Willie Mays ou Mickey Mantle. Aaron et Craig se tournent pour contempler la balle qui va mettre un terme au blanchissage du lanceur.

## "715," Atlanta Braves vs. Los Angeles Dodgers, April 8, 1974

**PAGES 154–155** Players from opposing teams are not supposed to congratulate each other, but some events are too historic to ignore. Dodgers shortstop Bill Russell (left) and second baseman Davey Lopes shake Hank Aaron's hand as he rounds the bases on the 715th home run of his career, breaking Babe Ruth's seemingly unbreakable record.

**SEITEN 154–155** Eigentlich sollten die Spieler ihrem Gegner nicht gratulieren, aber historische Ereignisse lassen sich nicht einfach ignorieren. Dodgers-Shortstop Bill Russell (l.) und Second Baseman Davey Lopes schütteln Hank Aaron die Hand, als der den 715. Homerun seiner Karriere feiert und den Rekord von Babe Ruth übertrumpft.

**PAGES 154–155** Des joueurs appartenant à des équipes adverses ne sont pas censés se congratuler. Et pourtant, certains événements historiques autorisent des entorses à la règle. Le bloqueur des Dodgers, Bill Russell (à gauche), et le deuxième base Davey Lopes serrent la main de Hank Aaron qui fait le tour des bases lors du 715ᵉ coup de circuit de sa carrière. Il pulvérise ainsi le record de Babe Ruth qui semblait jusqu'alors imbattable.

## Hank Aaron clowns, Atlanta Braves vs. Philadelphia Phillies

**OPPOSITE** Aaron (#44) entertains his teammates before a game by imitating an awful, off-balance batting stance, lifting his back foot and leaning forward awkwardly. The amused Braves include Ray Boone (#19), Mike Krsnich (#42), and fellow Hall of Famer Eddie Mathews (#41).

**GEGENÜBER** Aaron (44) unterhält vor einem Spiel seine Teamkameraden, indem er eine schlechte, wacklige Schlaghaltung imitiert, wobei er den hinteren Fuß hebt und sich unbeholfen vorbeugt. Unter den amüsierten Mitspielern: Ray Boone (19), Mike Krsnich (42) und Hall-of-Fame-Star Eddie Mathews (41).

**PAGE CI-CONTRE** Aaron (n° 44) distrait ses coéquipiers avant une rencontre. Il imite la position d'un batteur maladroit, à cloche-pied, déséquilibré vers l'avant. Parmi les Braves hilares: Ray Boone (n° 19), Mike Krsnich (n° 42) et un pair, membre du Temple de la renommée, Eddie Mathews (n° 41).

## A triumphant Aaron, Atlanta Braves vs. Los Angeles Dodgers, Atlanta Stadium, April 8, 1974

**RIGHT** After enduring hate mail and death threats from racists while chasing Babe Ruth's career home run record, Aaron was relieved as well as overjoyed to brandish the baseball he hit for the record-setting #715. *"I don't want them to forget Ruth,"* Aaron said. *"I just want them to remember me."*

**RECHTS** Hasserfüllte Briefe und Todesdrohungen von Rassisten hatten Aarons Jagd auf Babe Ruths Karriere-Rekord für Homeruns begleitet. Erleichtert und überglücklich schwingt Aaron nun den Ball, mit dem er den neuen Rekord aufgestellt hatte – seinen 715. Homerun. *„Ich will ja nicht, dass sie Ruth vergessen"*, sagte er, *„ich möchte nur, dass sie sich an mich erinnern."*

**A DROITE** Après avoir dû supporter les lettres d'insultes et les menaces de mort des racistes alors qu'il s'était lancé à la poursuite du record de coups de circuit établi par Babe Ruth, Aaron, soulagé et triomphant, brandit la balle qu'il a frappée pour son 715ᵉ home run. *« Je ne veux pas qu'on oublie Ruth »*, déclare Aaron. *« Je veux juste qu'on se souvienne de moi. »*

"He had about him the touch of royalty."

—Bowie Kuhn, eulogy for Roberto Clemente

**Roberto Clemente, right fielder, Pittsburgh Pirates, 1968**

**OPPOSITE** The first Latin American player elected to the Hall of Fame, Roberto Clemente left an even greater legacy as a humanitarian. The national hero of Puerto Rico died at 38 on New Year's Eve in 1972 when his plane, overloaded with supplies intended for earthquake victims in Nicaragua, crashed on takeoff. Clemente, right fielder for the Pittsburgh Pirates from 1954 to 1972, hit safely in all 14 World Series games he played in, earning MVP honors in the 1971 Series.

**GEGENÜBER** Roberto Clemente wurde als erster lateinamerikanischer Spieler in die Hall of Fame gewählt. Beinahe noch berühmter aber wurde er dadurch, dass er ein großes Herz für andere Menschen hatte. Der Nationalheld von Puerto Rico starb mit 38 am Silvesterabend 1972, als sein Flugzeug, überladen mit Hilfsgütern für die Opfer eines Erdbebens in Nicaragua, beim Start verunglückte.

Clemente, Right Fielder der Pittsburgh Pirates von 1954 bis 1972, hatte in jedem seiner 14 World-Series-Partien einen Treffer gelandet und wurde in der Series von 1971 zum besten Spieler gewählt.

**PAGE CI-CONTRE** Premier joueur latino-américain intronisé dans le Temple de la renommée, Roberto Clemente a laissé un héritage encore plus éclatant dans le domaine de l'humanitaire. Le héros national de Porto Rico est mort à trente-huit ans, le 31 décembre 1972, dans un accident aérien. Son avion, surchargé de vivres et de matériel destinés aux victimes d'un tremblement de terre au Nicaragua, s'est écrasé au décollage. Clemente, champ centre des Pittsburgh Pirates entre 1954 et 1972 a frappé des coups sûrs lors des quatorze World Series auxquelles il a participé. Il a en outre reçu le titre de MVP récompensant le meilleur joueur des Series de 1971.

## "The Great One," 1968

**OPPOSITE** Locked into his batting stance, poised for the pitch, Clemente glares defiantly at the opponent who imagines he can handle "The Great One" without difficulty. *"If I would be happy, I would be a very bad ball player,"* he said. *"With me, when I get mad, it puts energy in my body."*

**GEGENÜBER** Wie eingefroren in seiner Schlaghaltung wartet Clemente auf den Pitch und starrt dabei herausfordernd seinen Gegenspieler an, der glaubt, er werde ohne Probleme mit „The Great One" fertig werden. *„Wenn ich fröhlich wäre, wäre ich ein sehr schlechter Spieler"*, meinte Clemente. *„Aber wenn ich mich ärgere, dann verschafft mir das jede Menge Energie."*

**PAGE CI-CONTRE** Concentré sur sa position, immobile dans l'attente du lancer, Clemente défie du regard un adversaire qui croit pouvoir se défaire facilement de « The Great One ». *« Si j'étais joyeux, je serais un joueur médiocre »*, déclarait-il. *« Chez moi, la mauvaise humeur se transforme en énergie qui irradie tout mon corps. »*

## Roberto Clemente at bat, 1960 World Series

**RIGHT** Clemente steps into the pitch to lash another line drive. Hall of Fame pitcher Juan Marichal marveled, *"The big thing about Clemente is that he can hit any pitch. I don't mean only strikes. He can hit a ball off his ankles or off his ear."*

**RECHTS** Clemente geht in einen Wurf hinein und feuert einen weiteren flachen Ball ab. Hall-of-Fame-Pitcher Juan Marichal schwärmte: *„Das Tolle an Clemente ist, dass er jeden Wurf treffen kann. Also nicht nur normale Bälle, er trifft auch Bälle, die auf seine Füße oder seine Ohren zufliegen."*

**A DROITE** Clemente rentre dans la balle pour lâcher un nouveau coup en flèche. Le lanceur Juan Marichal, membre du Temple de la renommée, s'extasiait: *« Le plus étonnant chez Clemente, c'est qu'il est capable de contrer n'importe quel lancer. Je ne parle pas que des prises. Il pourrait renvoyer une balle avec ses chevilles ou son oreille. »*

### Clemente waits, Pittsburgh Pirates vs. St. Louis Cardinals, April 28, 1968

**LEFT** Not a slugger, Clemente was renowned as one of the best "bad ball" hitters ever, slashing at pitches out of the strike zone and whistling line drives to all parts of the field.

**LINKS** Clemente war kein Slugger, aber einer der besten „bad ball hitter" aller Zeiten, der Würfe außerhalb der Schlagzone als niedrige Schläge in alle Ecken des Platzes peitschte.

**A GAUCHE** Clemente qui n'était pas un frappeur, avait la réputation d'être l'un des meilleurs «bad ball hitters», c'est-à-dire qu'il attaquait toutes les balles y compris celles hors zone de prises et savait lâcher des coups en flèche partout sur le terrain.

### The grace of Clemente, 1968

**OPPOSITE** Clemente gracefully drifts under a fly ball. *"There are not enough TV pictures of him,"* laments Joe Brown, Pirates general manager during the Clemente era. *"He made so many great plays that people can only talk about."*

**GEGENÜBER** Locker und graziös verfolgt Clemente den hohen Flug des Balls. *„Es gibt nicht genug Fernsehbilder von ihm"*, klagt Joe Brown, General Manager der Pirates. *„Er hat so viele tolle Spiele gemacht, aber die Leute kennen sie nur vom Hörensagen."*

**PAGE CI-CONTRE** Clemente, toujours gracieux, suit une chandelle. *«Il ne reste pas assez d'images de lui»*, se lamente Joe Brown, manager général des Pirates. *«Il a accompli tellement d'exploits... malheureusement, on ne peut plus les voir, mais seulement en parler.»*

### In the locker room, 1968

**PAGES 164-165** Clemente does isotonic exercises with a spring, sophisticated equipment for 1968. Conditioning emphasized stretching and flexibility, unlike today's obsession with pure size and strength.

**SEITEN 164-165** Clemente macht isotonische Übungen mit einem Expander, einem 1968 noch ziemlich ausgefallenen Gerät. Im Gegensatz zur heutigen Obsession mit Krafttraining, Größe und Muskelkraft legte man damals beim Konditionstraining vor allem Wert auf Dehnübungen und Beweglichkeit.

**PAGES 164-165** Clemente pratique des contractions isométriques à l'aide d'un extenseur, appareil sophistiqué en 1968. L'entraînement mettait l'accent sur les étirements et la souplesse, contrairement aux exercices contemporains centrés sur les appareils de musculation. De nos jours, on est obsédé par la taille et la puissance.

**Pittsburgh Pirates vs. New York Yankees in World Series Game Two, Forbes Field, October 6, 1960**

**OPPOSITE** *"His Pirates teammates took goofy joy in watching Clemente run,"* wrote biographer David Maraniss. *"They would tell him he looked like a broken windmill, every limb rotating in a different direction. Clemente didn't actually run, they would say, he galloped."*

**GEGENÜBER** *„Seine Teamkameraden von den Pirates lachten sich schief, wenn Clemente lief",* schrieb sein Biograf David Maraniss. *„Sie lästerten, er sehe aus wie eine kaputte Windmühle, denn alle Gliedmaßen drehten sich in unterschiedliche Richtungen. Clemente, sagten sie, lief nicht, er galoppierte."*

**PAGE CI-CONTRE** *« Ses coéquipiers des Pirates tiraient une joie simple de le voir courir »,* a écrit son biographe David Maraniss. *« Ils lui disaient qu'il ressemblait à un moulin à vent cassé avec ses membres qui tournaient dans des directions opposées. En réalité, Clemente ne courait pas, affirmaient-ils... il galopait. »*

**Clemente prepares for a game, 1968**

**BELOW** Regarded as a hypochondriac, Clemente was beset by back, disc, and stomach problems. Also a proud man and a perfectionist, he believed he shouldn't play unless he could perform at 100% of his ability. Here he nurses an injured foot on the trainer's table, wondering whether he will be able to play that day.

**UNTEN** Clemente, der als Hypochonder galt, hatte ständig Probleme mit dem Rücken, der Bandscheibe und dem Magen. Aber er war auch ein stolzer Mann und ein Perfektionist und meinte, er solle nur spielen, wenn er wirklich 100 Prozent geben könne. Hier sitzt er mit einem verletzten Fuß auf dem Tisch des Masseurs und fragt sich, ob er am selben Tag wird spielen können.

**CI-DESSOUS** Considéré comme hypocondriaque, Clemente souffrait de problèmes de dos, de disques et d'estomac. Cependant, fier et perfectionniste, il croyait ne pas pouvoir jouer s'il n'était pas à cent pour cent de ses capacités. On le voit ici s'occuper d'un pied blessé sur la table du soigneur. Il se demande s'il pourra participer à la rencontre du jour.

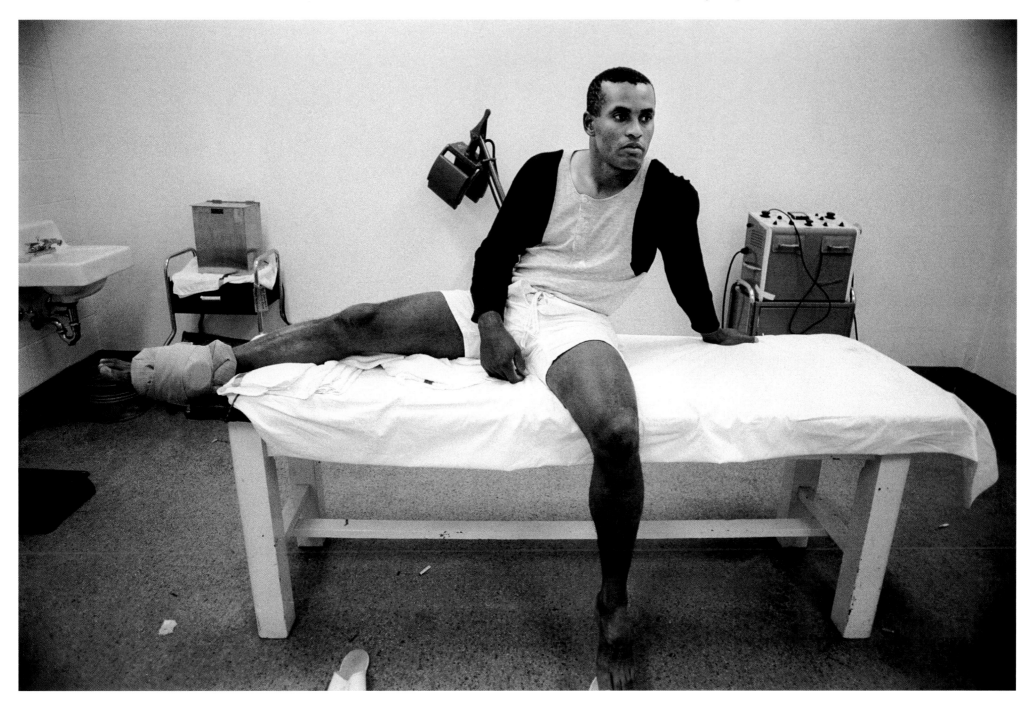

**Making contact, Pittsburgh Pirates vs. Chicago Cubs, Wrigley Field**

**BELOW** Roberto Clemente drills another base hit at Wrigley Field, his favorite place to hit apart from his home ballpark. Clemente's record shows that he hit better during day games than night games—and lights weren't installed at Wrigley until long after his career ended.

**UNTEN** Roberto Clemente schlägt einen Base Hit auf dem Wrigley Field, seinem Lieblingsplatz neben dem heimischen Stadion. Die Statistik besagt im Übrigen, dass Clemente bei Spielen am Tage besser schlug als abends – und Licht wurde in Wrigley erst lange nach dem Ende seiner Karriere installiert.

**CI-DESSOUS** Nouveau coup sûr de Clemente à Wrigley Field, son terrain favori à la batte après le stade des Pirates. Les statistiques de Clemente indiquent qu'il frappait mieux lors des rencontres de jour qu'au cours des parties en nocturnes. Ce n'est que bien après la fin de sa carrière que des projecteurs ont été installés à Wrigley.

## Clemente at practice, 1968

**BELOW** In *The Summer Game*, Roger Angell describes Clemente in batting practice: "*I saw Clemente step into the cage and take up an unnatural stance, with his legs and feet together. Frozen like that, and swinging only from the waist up, merely getting his eye in, he lined the next three pitches successively to right, to center, and to left—pop, pop, pop—all hits in any game.*"

**UNTEN** In *The Summer Game* beschreibt Roger Angell Clemente beim Schlagtraining: „*Ich sah, wie Clemente ins Schlaggitter stieg und eine unnatürliche Position einnahm. Er stand da wie festgenagelt, nahm nur mit dem Oberkörper Schwung und feuerte die nächsten drei Würfe erfolgreich nach rechts, in die Mitte, nach links – bum, bum, bum –, in jedem Spiel wären das Treffer gewesen.*"

**CI-DESSOUS** Dans *The Summer Game*, Roger Angell décrit Clemente pendant l'entraînement des batteurs: «*J'ai vu Clemente entrer dans le tunnel de frappe et adopter une position curieuse, les jambes et les pieds joints. Ainsi figé, son corps ne bougeait qu'au-dessus de la taille. Il a lancé les trois balles suivantes à droite, puis au centre et enfin à gauche – pop, pop, pop. Il aurait réussi des coups sûrs dans n'importe quelle partie.* »

"When a pitcher's throwing a spitball, don't worry and don't complain, just hit the dry side like I do."
—Stan Musial

**Stan Musial, outfielder, St. Louis Cardinals, 1963**

**OPPOSITE** As Commissioner Ford Frick put it on the day Stan Musial retired, *"Here stands baseball's happy warrior; here stands baseball's perfect knight."* For more than two decades he was the class of the National League, winning seven batting titles. *"He was good enough to take your breath away,"* said broadcaster Vin Scully. Musial anchored the St. Louis Cardinals offense from 1942 to 1963, winning seven batting titles, topping the .350 mark five times, and amassing 3,630 hits—the fourth-highest career total.

**GEGENÜBER** Ford Frick, der Vorsitzende der Major League Baseball, hatte schon recht, als er bei Stan Musials Rücktritt sagte: *„Hier steht Baseballs glücklicher Krieger, hier steht Baseballs perfekter Ritter."* Mehr als zwei Jahrzehnte lang war er in der National League eine Klasse für sich. *„Er war so gut, dass es einem den Atem verschlug"*, sagte der Rundfunkreporter Vin Scully. Musial war eine Stütze für die Offensive der St. Louis Cardinals von 1942 bis 1963, gewann siebenmal den Titel bester Schlagmann, übertraf fünfmal die .350-Marke und kam insgesamt auf 3.630 Treffer – die vierthöchste Zahl für eine Spielerlaufbahn.

**PAGE CI-CONTRE** Le jour où Stan Musial a pris sa retraite, le président de la Ligue majeure, Ford Frick, a déclaré: *« Ici se tient le guerrier joyeux du base-ball ; ici se tient le preux chevalier du base-ball. »* Pendant plus de deux décennies, il a tenu le haut du panier dans la Ligue nationale et a remporté sept titres à la batte. *« Tellement bon, qu'il vous coupait le souffle »*, disait de lui le commentateur Vin Scully. Musial a été la pierre angulaire de l'attaque des Cardinals entre 1942 et 1963: il a atteint cinq fois une moyenne de 0.350 et a cumulé 3 630 coups sûrs, soit le quatrième meilleur total de carrière.

"In the end it all comes down to talent ... Can nice guys win? Sure, nice guys can win—if they're nice guys with a lot of talent."

—Sandy Koufax

# "Pitching is the art of instilling fear."
## —Sandy Koufax

**The rivalry turns violent, Los Angeles Dodgers vs. San Francisco Giants, Candlestick Park, August 22, 1965**

**PAGE 191** Juan Marichal became enraged at Dodgers catcher John Roseboro for whistling the ball past his ear when returning it to pitcher Sandy Koufax. Marichal whacked Roseboro over the head with his bat, then raised it to bludgeon Roseboro again as he fell to the ground.

**SEITE 191** Juan Marichal darüber ärgerte, dass Dodgers-Fänger John Roseboro den Ball knapp an seinem Ohr vorbei zu Pitcher Sandy Koufax zurückwarf. Er haute Roseboro das Schlagholz über den Kopf und holte schon zum zweiten Schlag aus, als der zu Boden ging.

**PAGE 191** Juan Marichal s'énerve contre le receveur des Dodgers, John Roseboro, qui lui a frôlé l'oreille en renvoyant la balle au lanceur, Sandy Koufax. Marichal finit par le frapper à la tête avec sa batte. Il la lève une seconde fois tandis que Roseboro s'écroule.

**Frank Finch, Los Angeles Times reporter:**

**PAGES 192–193** *"Capt. [Willie] Mays twice helped restrain the enraged Roseboro from getting back at Marichal, and in a touching tableau Willie tenderly wiped blood from Roseboro's forehead."*

**SEITEN 192–193** *„Kapitän [Willie] Mays half zweimal mit, den wütenden Roseboro daran zu hindern, nun seinerseits auf Marichal loszugehen, und wischte ihm in einer rührenden Szene zärtlich das Blut von der Stirn."*

**PAGES 192–193** *« Le capitaine [Willie] Mays a aidé deux fois à retenir Roseboro qui voulait prendre sa revanche sur Marichal. Tableau émouvant, Willie a essuyé tendrement le sang qui coulait du front de Roseboro. »*

**Two immortals square off, Los Angeles Dodgers vs. San Francisco Giants, Candlestick Park, August 22, 1965**

**OPPOSITE** Koufax reaches the apex of his delivery before unleashing a fastball to Willie Mays. Mays flied out to center fielder Willie Davis (background) this time, but after the Marichal-Roseboro incident hit a three-run homer off a rattled Koufax that proved the game-winner.

**GEGENÜBER** Koufax setzt gerade dazu an, einen scharfen Ball in Richtung Willie Mays abzufeuern. Diesmal schlug Mays einen Flugball zu Center Fielder Willie Davis (im Hintergrund), im nächsten Inning aber, nach dem Marichal-Roseboro-Zwischenfall, nahm er einem nervösen Koufax einen Drei-Punkte-Homerun ab, was schließlich das Spiel entschied.

**PAGE CI-CONTRE** Koufax, à l'acmé de sa préparation, est photographié juste avant de catapulter une balle rapide à Willie Mays. Willie Davis, le champ centre (au fond), interceptera la balle de volée. Après l'incident ayant opposé Marichal à Roseboro, et devant un Koufax déconcerté, Mays va frapper un coup de circuit à trois points qui apportera la victoire à son équipe.

### "The Duke" swings, Los Angeles Dodgers, circa 1960

**LEFT** Twisted like a pretzel, Edwin "Duke" Snider follows through after a big swing. Snider remains the underrated member of the celebrated "Willie, Mickey, and The Duke" trio of 1950s New York center fielders, but nobody hit more home runs during that decade than he did.

**LINKS** Mit buchstäblich verknoteten Beinen zieht Edwin „Duke" Snider nach einem gewaltigen Schwung durch. Obwohl niemand in jenem Jahrzehnt mehr Homeruns schlug als er, wird Snider von den Dreien des berühmten New Yorker Outfielder-Trio „Willie, Mickey und Duke" immer noch unterbewertet.

**A GAUCHE** Entortillé tel un bretzel, Edwin « Duke » Snider accompagne une frappe. Dans les années cinquante, Snider est demeuré le membre le moins estimé du trio de joueurs de champ extérieur « Willie, Mickey et le Duke ». Pourtant, personne n'a surpassé le nombre de coups de circuit frappés par Snider durant cette décennie.

### Marichal on the mound, Los Angeles Dodgers vs. San Francisco Giants, Candlestick Park, August 22, 1965

**OPPOSITE** Willie Davis of the Dodgers tries to keep his eye on the ball as Juan Marichal strides toward the plate, leaning to gain leverage, face straining with the effort of pitching.

**GEGENÜBER** Willie Davis von den Dodgers versucht, den Ball im Blick zu halten, während sich auf Juan Marichals Gesicht die Anstrengung spiegelt, als er sich zurücklehnt, um kraftvoll auszuholen.

**PAGE CI-CONTRE** Willie Davis des Dodgers essaie de garder un œil sur la balle tandis que Juan Marichal, sur le marbre, se penche pour gagner de la puissance, le visage tendu par l'effort produit pour le lancer.

## High and inside, New York Yankees vs. Boston Red Sox, 1976

**OPPOSITE AND RIGHT** Mickey Rivers backs away from a high-and-inside fastball, the pitch that gives catcher Carlton Fisk the best chance to gun down a runner attempting to steal a base, because it keeps the batter from leaning across the plate to interfere (legally) with the throw. Despite Fisk's quick release, Sandy Alomar stole the base, and Rivers singled him in to tie the game at 2-2.

**GEGENÜBER UND RECHTS** Mickey Rivers weicht vor einem hohen Fastball zurück, einem Wurf, der Fänger Carlton Fisk eine sehr gute Chance gibt, einen Läufer beim Stehlen eines Base zu erwischen, weil dieser Wurf es dem Schlagmann unmöglich macht, sich über das Mal hinauszulehnen und (legal) an den Wurf zu gelangen. Aber obwohl Fisk den Ball blitzschnell wieder loslässt, stiehlt Sandy Alomar das Base, und Rivers ermöglicht ihm einen Run, womit er das Spiel zum 2:2 ausgleicht.

**PAGE CI-CONTRE ET À DROITE** Mickey Rivers recule devant une balle rapide haute. Un tel lancer donne une chance certaine au receveur Carlton Fisk de pouvoir éliminer un coureur tentant de voler une base car il empêche le batteur de se pencher au-dessus de la base afin d'interférer (légalement) avec la balle. Malgré le relais rapide de Fisk, Sandy Alomar vole la base. Rivers lui permet de marquer sur un simple et d'égaliser 2-2.

**Don Drysdale winds up, Los Angeles Dodgers vs. San Francisco Giants, Candlestick Park, August 19, 1965**

**PAGES 200-201** Like a hawk spotting its prey, six-foot-five Drysdale spreads his wingspan wide and prepares to swoop down on a Giants batter. Drysdale battled the enemy for a dozen tough innings before yielding to the bullpen in a game the Dodgers finally won in 15 innings.

**SEITEN 200-201** Wie ein Habicht über seiner Beute breitet der über 1,95 Meter große Don Drysdale seine Arme weit aus für einen Sturzflug auf einen Schlagmann der Giants. Drysdale schlug sich zwölf schwere Innings lang mit dem Gegner, bevor er sich ablösen ließ. Die Dodgers gewannen am Ende in 15 Innings.

**PAGES 200-201** Tel le faucon ayant repéré sa proie, Don Drysdale, un mètre quatre-vingt-quinze, se déploie et se prépare à fondre sur le batteur des Giants. Drysdale va affronter l'ennemi pendant une douzaine de manches serrées avant de laisser la place au lanceur de relève. Les Dodgers remporteront finalement la victoire en quinze manches.

**Drysdale despondent, Los Angeles Dodgers vs. San Francisco Giants in Playoff Game Three, Dodger Stadium, October 3, 1962**

**BELOW** A despondent Don Drysdale is oblivious to a reporter's question following his Dodgers' collapse in the final playoff game. Drysdale had his best season in 1962, winning 25 games, but his own glory couldn't ease the emptiness of watching a four-run ninth inning lift the hated Giants to a comeback victory and a spot in the World Series.

**UNTEN** Don Drysdale ist so niedergeschlagen, dass er den Reporter, der ihn nach dem Aus seiner Dodgers im letzten Playoffspiel interviewen will, gar nicht bemerkt. 1962 war seine beste Saison mit 25 Siegen, aber auch der eigene Ruhm konnte die Leere nicht wettmachen, die er empfand, als die verhassten Giants im neunten Inning mit einem Run über vier Bases noch zum Sieg und damit in die World Series kamen.

**CI-DESSOUS** Don Drysdale, déprimé, ne répond pas aux questions posées par un journaliste après la défaite des Dodgers dans la dernière rencontre des play-offs. Drysdale connaît sa meilleure saison en 1962, en gagnant vingt-cinq matchs. Toutefois, ses victoires personnelles ne peuvent combler le désespoir provoqué par le retour gagnant des Giants honnis grâce à un coup à quatre points marqué dans la neuvième manche.

**A light moment, Los Angeles Dodgers vs. San Francisco Giants, Candlestick Park, August 20, 1965**

**OPPOSITE** After a 15-inning dogfight the night before, team captains Maury Wills of the Dodgers (left) and Willie Mays of the Giants are all smiles as they exchange lineup cards during the pre-game ritual with the umpiring crew. Two days later the smiles vanished in the wake of the Marichal-Roseboro fracas.

**GEGENÜBER** Nach einer endlosen Schlacht über 15 Innings am Vorabend strahlen die Mannschaftsführer Maury Wills von den Dodgers (l.) und Willie Mays von den Giants übers ganze Gesicht, als sie vor dem Spiel die Aufstellungen mit den Schiedsrichtern austauschen. Zwei Tage später, nach dem Marichal-Roseboro-Tumult, war ihnen das Lachen vergangen.

**PAGE CI-CONTRE** Après quinze manches d'une lutte serrée, la veille, les capitaines Maury Wills (Dodgers, à gauche) et Willie Mays (Giants) se sourient en échangeant les feuilles d'ordre à la batte durant le rituel d'avant match et sous l'œil attentif de l'équipe arbitrale. Deux jours plus tard, les sourires auront disparu en raison de la rixe Marichal-Roseboro.

**Collision at the plate, New York Yankees vs. Boston Red Sox, Yankee Stadium, May 20, 1976**

**PAGES 204-205** The bodies fly in opposite directions as Jim Rice of the Red Sox slides into home plate. Yankees catcher Thurman Munson sprawls on his side to make the tag on Rice, who tried to score on a ground ball to the shortstop. Umpire Terry Cooney monitors the traffic at his feet and prepares to make the call.

**SEITEN 204-205** Als Jim Rice von den Red Sox zum Schlagmal rutscht, während Yankee-Fänger Thurman Munson auf der Seite liegt, um Rice abzuklatschen, der versucht, mit einem auf den Boden geschlagenen Ball zum Shortstop zu punkten, rutschen die beiden in entgegengesetzte Richtungen. Schiedsrichter Terry Cooney verfolgt das Geschehen und wird gleich seine Entscheidung fällen.

**PAGES 204-205** Les corps semblent voler dans des directions opposées. Jim Rice des Red Sox glisse vers le marbre. Le receveur des Yankees, Thurman Munson, essaie de rouler sur lui-même pour toucher Rice qui tente de marquer sur un roulant expédié en direction du bloqueur. L'arbitre Terry Cooney surveille ce qui se passe à ses pieds et réfléchit à sa décision.

**Tagged out, Los Angeles Dodgers vs. San Francisco Giants, Candlestick Park, August 19, 1965**

**OPPOSITE AND BELOW** Umpire Tony Venzon does a little jig to avoid a collision as he calls Willie Crawford of the Dodgers out at home plate. Crawford tried to score the winning run from third base in the 12th inning on a tapper to the mound, but pitcher Gaylord Perry (background) tossed the ball to catcher Tom Haller in time to nail Crawford. It took the Dodgers 15 innings to win this battle.

**GEGENÜBER UND UNTEN** Schiedsrichter Tony Venzon macht eine kleine Tanzeinlage, um einen Zusammenstoß zu vermeiden, als er am Schlagmal auf „out" für Willie Crawford von den Dodgers entscheidet. Crawford versuchte, den entscheidenden Run im 12. Inning vom dritten Base mit einem langsamen Ball zum Wurfmal zu erreichen, aber Pitcher Gaylord Perry (im Hintergrund) warf den Ball rechtzeitig zu Fänger Tom Haller, um Crawford zu erwischen. Für den Sieg in dieser Schlacht gegen die Giants brauchten die Dodgers 15 Innings.

**PAGE CI-CONTRE ET CI-DESSOUS** Douzième manche: petite danse de l'arbitre Tony Venzon pour éviter une collision. Il annonce l'élimination sur le marbre de Willie Crawford des Dodgers. Crawford a essayé de marquer le point de la victoire en partant de la troisième base sur un roulant apathique. Le lanceur Gaylord Perry (au fond) a relayé la balle au receveur Tom Haller à temps pour coincer Crawford. Il faudra quinze manches aux Dodgers pour gagner cette bataille contre les Giants.

**Allow me to explain myself, New York Yankees vs. Boston Red Sox, Yankee Stadium, May 21, 1976**

**BELOW AND OPPOSITE** *"What do you expect me to do about it? I already made my call,"* the umpires seem to be saying as they face the carping combatants in another Yankees-Red Sox battle. On the left, Red Sox coach Don Zimmer (#34) and Rick Burleson protest a crucial double-play call; on the right and opposite, Yankees manager Billy Martin is outraged as usual.

**UNTEN UND GEGENÜBER** *„Was erwarten Sie von mir? Ich habe meine Entscheidung getroffen"*, scheinen die Schiedsrichter den meckernden Kämpfern der Yankees und der Red Sox zu sagen. Links protestieren Red-Sox-Trainer Don Zimmer (34) und Rick Burleson gegen die Entscheidung in einem wichtigen Double Play, rechts und gegenüber ist Yankee-Trainer Billy Martin wie immer außer sich.

**CI-DESSOUS ET PAGE CI-CONTRE** *« Qu'est-ce que vous voulez que j'y fasse ? J'ai déjà pris ma décision »*, semblent s'excuser les arbitres face aux joueurs mécontents des Yankees et des Red Sox. À gauche, l'entraîneur des Red Sox, Don Zimmer (n° 34) et Rick Burleson contestent la décision sur un double jeu ; à droite, le manager des Yankees, Billy Martin, est outré... comme d'habitude.

## Walt Alston and Herman Franks

**PAGES 210–213** After a tough loss, the last thing a manager wants to do is face the inquisitive press, but it's part of the job. Herman Franks of the Giants (pages 210–211) makes his stand after Marichal's attack on John Roseboro. Dodgers manager Walter Alston (pages 212–213) gets some solace from a cigarette as he tries to explain why his ace, Sandy Koufax, got knocked out in the second inning of the crucial first playoff game against the Giants in 1962.

**SEITEN 210–213** Was ein Trainer nach einer bitteren Niederlage am wenigsten schätzt, sind die bohrenden Fragen der Presse. Aber das ist Teil des Jobs. Herman Franks von den Giants (S. 210–211) äußert sich nach Marichals Angriff auf John Roseboro. Mit einer Zigarette versucht sich Dodgers-Trainer Walter Alston

(S. 212–213) zu trösten, als er zu erklären versucht, warum sein Star, Sandy Koufax, im zweiten Inning des wichtigen ersten Playoffspiels gegen die Giants 1962 geschlagen worden war.

**PAGES 210–213** Après avoir subi une défaite sévère, la dernière chose qu'un manager souhaite, c'est affronter une presse inquisitrice... et pourtant, cela fait partie du boulot. Herman Franks des Giants (pages 210-211) se justifie après l'agression de Marichal contre John Roseboro. Le manager des Dodgers, Walter Alston (pages 212-213) essaie de tirer un certain réconfort de sa cigarette tout en expliquant pourquoi son lanceur vedette, Sandy Koufax, a été retiré du jeu dans la seconde manche de la première partie cruciale des play-offs contre les Giants en 1962.

## Los Angeles Dodgers vs. San Francisco Giants, Candlestick Park, August 20, 1965

**OPPOSITE** Major league baseball had emphasized pitching and home runs for two decades before Maury Wills came along and changed the game. In 1962, he was the National League's MVP despite hitting only six home runs. He stole 104 bases, ushering in a fresh emphasis on speed.

**GEGENÜBER** Pitchen und Homeruns waren zwei Jahrzehnte lang das Wichtigste im Profi-Baseball – bis Maury Wills auf der Bühne erschien und das Spiel veränderte. 1962 wurde er der wertvollste Spieler der National League, obwohl er nur

sechs Homeruns geschlagen hatte. Aber er stahl 104 Bases – und fortan wurde Schnelligkeit zu einem der wichtigsten Merkmale.

**PAGE CI-CONTRE** Le baseball en ligue majeure a mis l'accent pendant deux décennies sur le lancer et les coups de circuit. Et puis Maury Wills est arrivé et il a transformé le jeu. En 1962, il est élu Most Valuable Player (meilleur joueur) alors qu'il n'a frappé que six « home runs ». Mais il a volé cent quatre bases et il a inauguré une nouvelle époque : celle de la vitesse.

## New York Yankees vs. Boston Red Sox, Yankee Stadium, May 20, 1976

**PAGES 215-223** Two pugnacious rivals head for trouble as Lou Piniella of the Yankees tries to score from second base on a single, with catcher Carlton Fisk waiting for him. Baseball chronicler Roger Angell wrote that *"the crash—the most violent plate collision I have ever seen—knocked both players sprawling, and instantly set off a prolonged and extremely ugly fight."*

**SEITEN 215-223** Gleich werden zwei rauflustige Gegenspieler aneinander geraten, wenn Yankee Lou Piniella versucht, vom Second Base aus direkt zu punkten, während Fänger Carlton Fisk schon auf ihn wartet. Der Baseball-Chronist Roger Angell schrieb: *„Der Zusammenstoß – die bru-*

*talste Kollision, die ich je am Schlagmal gesehen habe – zwang beide Spieler zu Boden und führte sofort zu einem langen und äußerst hässlichen Kampf."*

**PAGES 215-223** Deux rivaux pugnaces se jettent tête baissée dans les ennuis. Lou Piniella des Yankees essaie de marquer sur un simple depuis la deuxième base, mais le receveur Carlton Fisk l'attend. Le chroniqueur sportif, spécialiste du baseball, Roger Angell a écrit que *« le choc – la collision la plus violente que j'aie jamais vue sur une base – a étalé les deux joueurs de tout leur long. Une bagarre navrante et plutôt violente s'est immédiatement déclenchée. Elle a duré un certain temps. »*

**The Aftermath, New York Yankees vs. Boston Red Sox, Yankee Stadium, May 20, 1976**

**PAGES 215-223** The only casualty in the melee was Red Sox pitcher Bill Lee, being led away by trainer Charlie Moss. *"I ran in the first time to try and break up Piniella and Fisk,"* said Graig Nettles of the Yankees. *"There was Lee on top of them, so I grabbed him around the arms and body and pulled him off. He fell on his shoulder."*

**SEITEN 215-223** Der einzige Verletzte in dieser Schlägerei war Red-Sox-Pitcher Bill Lee, der von Trainer Charlie Moss vom Platz geleitet wird. *„Ich bin da zunächst nur reingegangen, um Piniella und Fisk zu trennen"*, sagte Graig Nettles von den Yankees. *„Aber Lee lag schon über ihnen, also habe ich ihn bei den Armen und am Körper gegriffen und heruntergezogen. Dabei fiel er auf die Schulter."*

**PAGES 215-223** Seul blessé dans la mêlée générale, Bill Lee, le lanceur des Red Sox, est escorté par l'entraîneur Charlie Moss. *« J'ai accouru pour essayer de séparer Piniella et Fisk »*, a affirmé Graig Nettles des Yankees. *« Il y avait Lee par-dessus, alors je l'ai saisi par les bras et je l'ai tiré. Il est tombé sur son épaule. »*

**On deck, Los Angeles Dodgers vs. San Francisco Giants in Playoff Game Two, Dodger Stadium, October 2, 1962**

**BELOW** With the score tied in the final inning, slugger Duke Snider waits to bat next. But sometimes even a Hall of Famer isn't needed. The batter, Jim Gilliam, walked, setting up a bunt situation. Snider yielded to pinch-hitter Daryl Spencer, a better bunter. The strategy worked, leading to the winning run.

**UNTEN** Unentschieden im letzten Inning und Slugger Duke Snider ist der nächste Schlagmann. Aber manchmal braucht's keinen Hall-of-Fame-Star: Snider verzichtete zugunsten von Reserve-Schlagmann Daryl Spencer, der ein besserer „bunter" war und dessen Schlag tatsächlich zum entscheidenden Run führte.

**CI-DESSOUS** Égalité dans la dernière manche, Duke Snider, un cogneur, attend son tour à la batte. Cependant, certains jours, on n'a pas besoin d'un membre du Temple de la renommée. Le batteur, Jim Gilliam, bénéficie d'une base automatique. Snider va donc céder la place au frappeur d'urgence, Daryl Spencer, meilleur frappeur. La stratégie fonctionne et mène l'équipe à la victoire.

## Marichal high-kicking, August 1965

**RIGHT** Juan Marichal had to be a fantastic athlete just to execute this unique high-kicking windup on every pitch without falling over. Despite the increased leverage gained from throwing two limbs to the sky and dipping the ball almost to the ground, Marichal was known more for his pinpoint control than his velocity.

**RECHTS** Juan Marichal war ein fabelhafter Athlet: Vor jedem Wurf stieg er hoch in die Luft, ohne hinzufallen. Zusätzliche Hebelwirkung gewann er, indem er Arm und Bein gen Himmel streckte und mit dem Ball fast den Boden berührte. Trotzdem war er eher für die absolute Genauigkeit seiner Würfe bekannt als für deren Schnelligkeit.

**À DROITE** Juan Marichal se devait d'être un athlète formidable ne serait-ce que pour exécuter cette préparation de lancer acrobatique... sans tomber. En projetant bras et jambes gauches vers le ciel et en amenant la balle presque au sol, il gagnait de la puissance. Toutefois, Marichal est plus connu pour sa précision que pour la vélocité de son lancer.

**At the head, Los Angeles Dodgers vs. San Francisco Giants, Candlestick Park, July 5, 1962**

**OPPOSITE** Willie Mays gracefully arches away from a high-inside fastball intended by Dodgers pitcher Johnny Podres to intimidate the batter. Mays had the last laugh on this day, however, belting a home run off Podres to lead the Giants to a 10-3 victory.

**GEGENÜBER** Elegant geht Schlagmann Willie Mays einem hohen Fastball aus dem Weg, mit dem Dodgers-Pitcher Johnny Podres ihn einschüchtern wollte. Mays lachte an diesem Tag als Letzter, er erzielte einen Homerun gegen Podres und führte die Giants zum 10:3-Sieg.

**PAGE CI-CONTRE** Willie Mays évite gracieusement une balle rapide intérieure expédiée par le lanceur des Dodgers Johnny Podres dans l'optique d'intimider le batteur. Mais rira bien qui rira le dernier... Mays, ce jour-là, va frapper un coup de circuit sur un lancer de Podres qui donnera la victoire aux Giants, 10-3.

**At the shins, San Francisco Giants vs. Los Angeles Dodgers, Candlestick Park, July 5, 1962**

**BELOW** There's more than one way to skin a cat. Pitchers don't always throw at the batter's head to back him off the plate. It's just as effective to aim at his shins, as Johnny Podres does here, forcing the batter to jack-knife out of the way and giving him one more thing to worry about as he digs in for the next pitch.

**UNTEN** Viele Wege führen nach Rom. Pitcher müssen nicht immer auf den Kopf des Schlagmannes zielen, um ihn vom Schlagmal zu vertreiben. Ebenso effektiv ist es, aufs Schien-bein zu zielen, so wie Johnny Podres hier. Noch während er sich mit einem Hechtsprung in Sicherheit bringt, muss sich der Schlagmann um den nächsten Wurf sorgen.

**CI-DESSOUS** Il y a plusieurs façons de plumer un canard. Les lanceurs ne visent pas forcément la tête pour faire reculer le batteur. Il est tout aussi efficace de cibler les tibias, comme Johnny Podres ici, qui oblige le batteur à sauter comme un cabri pour éviter l'impact. À la balle suivante, le lanceur a l'avantage psychologique.

**"You're out!" Los Angeles Dodgers vs. San Francisco Giants, Candlestick Park, August 22, 1965**

**BELOW** Getting called out on strikes will make any batter fume, but when the tying run is on base in the ninth inning and the strikeout ends the game, it is doubly enraging. Jim Gilliam of the Dodgers screams his protest as umpire Shag Crawford "rings him up" and Giants catcher Dick Bertell starts to celebrate.

**UNTEN** Wenn man als Schlagmann ins Out geschickt wird, weil man sich dreimal einen „strike" geleistet, also drei in die Schlagzone geworfene Bälle nicht getroffen hat, ist das schon Grund genug, wütend zu werden. Aber wenn ein Strikeout im neunten Inning kurz vor dem Ausgleich das Spiel beendet, ist das doppelt ärgerlich. Jim Gillian von den Dodgers schreit seinen Protest heraus, als Schiedsrichter Shag Crawford ihn auszählt, während Giants-Fänger Dick Bertell schon feiert.

**CI-DESSOUS** Être éliminé sur trois prises enrage tous les batteurs, mais quand il s'agit de la neuvième manche et qu'il y avait possibilité de marquer le point de la victoire... il y a vraiment de quoi râler. Jim Gilliam des Dodgers proteste avec véhémence contre l'arbitre Shag Crawford qui signale son retrait. Le receveur des Giants, Dick Bertell, se précipite vers ses coéquipiers pour fêter la victoire.

**Top of the ninth, Los Angeles Dodgers vs. San Francisco Giants in Playoff Game Three, Dodger Stadium, October 3, 1962**

**OPPOSITE** It's the ninth inning, and if the Dodgers can hold their 4-2 lead they'll win the playoff and the National League pennant and go on to the World Series. Giants batter Harvey Kuenn grounds out, and pitcher Ed Roebuck has the first of three needed outs. That's the only one he'll get, however, as two walks and a single knock him out of the game.

**GEGENÜBER** Neuntes Inning. Wenn die Dodgers ihren 4:2-Vorsprung halten, haben sie die Playoffs und die Meisterschaft der National League gewonnen und erreichen die World Series. Giants-Schlagmann Harvey Kuenn patzt und Pitcher Ed Roebuck erreicht das erste von drei erforderlichen Outs. Aber es bleibt auch das einzige, denn nach zwei gegnerischen Walks und einem Schlag aufs erste Base ist das Spiel für ihn zu Ende.

**PAGE CI-CONTRE** Neuvième manche: si les Dodgers parviennent à maintenir leur avance – ils mènent 4-2 – ils gagneront les play-offs, le titre de la Ligue nationale, et participeront aux World Series. Le batteur des Giants Harvey Kuenn est éliminé sur un roulant intercepté. Ed Roebuck, le lanceur, aurait besoin de sortir deux joueurs supplémentaires. Il n'y arrivera pas. Il sera remplacé après avoir accordé deux bases automatiques et un simple à ses adversaires.

"The people of Boston live in silent dread of the Yankees. Whenever the Red Sox prepared to play the Yankees, it was as if they were dressing up for battle ... We knew we were getting ready to take the field and up-hold our values, as though we were knights in armor. That's how I felt. And I wasn't alone."

—*Bill "Spaceman" Lee*, THE WRONG STUFF, 1984

**Bases loaded, Los Angeles Dodgers vs. San Francisco Giants in Playoff Game Three, Dodger Stadium, October 3, 1962**

**OPPOSITE** Three batters after Harvey Kuenn's out, Willie Mays delivers a bases-loaded single, his only hit in the deciding playoff game, to drive in the first run in a four-run rally that lifts the Giants from the brink of defeat to the National League pennant.

**GEGENÜBER** Als drittem Schlagmann nach dem Aus für Harvey Kuenn gelingt Willie Mays ein Schlag mit drei besetzten Bases, sein einziger Treffer im entscheidenden Playoff-spiel und der erste in einer 4-Punkte-Aufholjagd, die die Giants vom Rand der Niederlage zur Meisterschaft der National League führt.

**PAGE CI-CONTRE** Trois batteurs après l'élimination d'Harvey Kuenn, Willie Mays expédie un simple sur bases pleines, son seul coup sûr lors de la rencontre décisive des play-offs. Il marque le premier point d'une remontée qui en comptera quatre et fera passer les Giants du bord du gouffre... au titre de la Ligue nationale.

"Baseball is really two sports — the Summer Game and the Autumn Game. One is the leisurely pastime of our national mythology. The other is not so gentle."

—*Thomas Boswell, HOW LIFE IMITATES THE WORLD SERIES,* 1983

## Yogi Berra, New York Yankees vs. Pittsburgh Pirates in World Series Game Seven, Forbes Field, October 13, 1960

**PAGE 233** The follow-through of a home run swing shows how the lower body and hip rotation generate much of a batter's power. Yogi Berra follows the trajectory of a three-run blast that briefly gave his Yankees the lead, while Pirates catcher Smoky Burgess slumps at the realization that his team has just lost it.

**SEITE 233** Beim Durchziehen eines Homerun-Schlages kann man erkennen, wie der Schlagmann die Kraft aus der Drehung von Unterkörper und Hüfte gewinnt. Yogi Berra verfolgt die Flugbahn eines gewaltigen Schlages für den sicheren Drei-Punkte-Homerun, der die Yankees kurzzeitig in Führung bringt, während Pirates-Fänger Smoky Burgess resigniert, als er erkennt, dass seine Mannschaft gerade die Führung eingebüßt hat.

**PAGE 233** Importance de l'accompagnement dans un coup de circuit: la photographie montre comment la puissance du batteur est générée en grande partie par le mouvement du bas du corps et notamment par la rotation des hanches. Yogi Berra suit la trajectoire d'un formidable coup à trois points qui va brièvement faire passer les Yankees en tête. Smoky Burgess, le receveur des Pirates, s'effondre en voyant s'envoler l'avantage de son équipe.

## Boston takes the field, Boston Red Sox vs. St. Louis Cardinals in World Series Game One, Fenway Park, October 4, 1967

**OPPOSITE** A magical moment at any ballgame comes when the home team dashes en masse from the dugout to their defensive positions to start the game. Here, the Red Sox take the field for their first World Series game in 21 years, ending two decades of anticipation and beginning a new chapter in baseball history.

**GEGENÜBER** Es ist stets ein magischer Augenblick, wenn die Heimmannschaft zu Beginn des Spiels aus dem Graben stürmt und ihre Verteidigungspositionen einnimmt. Hier laufen die Red Sox für ihrer erstes World-Series-Spiel in 21 Jahren auf – Ende von zwei Jahrzehnten der Erwartung und Beginn eines neues Kapitels der Baseballgeschichte.

**PAGE CI-CONTRE** Un moment magique lors de chaque rencontre de base-ball: l'équipe qui reçoit sort des vestiaires et se précipite vers ses positions défensives afin de commencer la partie. Ici, les Red Sox investissent le terrain pour leurs premières World Series en vingt et un ans. Ils mettent ainsi fin à deux décennies d'attente et inaugurent un nouveau chapitre de l'histoire du base-ball.

**Los Angeles Dodgers vs. Minnesota Twins in World Series Game Five, Dodger Stadium, October 11, 1965**

**OPPOSITE** The prime intersection of fielders and runners, second base is the center for baseball acrobatics. Shortstop Zoilo Versalles of the Twins sails across the base to spear a wild pickoff throw while Dick Tracewski ducks for cover and umpire Eddie Hurley leans in to make the call.

**GEGENÜBER** Das Second Base, wo Feldspieler und Läufer am häufigsten aufeinander treffen, ist der Schauplatz für Baseball-Akrobatik. Twins-Shortstop Zoilo Versalles segelt über das Base, um einen wilden Pickoff-Wurf zu erreichen, während Dick Tracewski sich wegduckt und Schiedsrichter Eddie Hurley genau hinsieht, um eine Entscheidung zu treffen.

**PAGE CI-CONTRE** Passage obligé des coureurs et des joueurs de champ, la deuxième base est le théâtre de la plupart des acrobaties au base-ball. Le bloqueur Zoilo Versalles des Twins s'envole pour attraper un relais sur base tandis que Dick Tracewski se met à l'abri. L'arbitre Eddie Hurley se penche afin de prendre la bonne décision.

**Cincinnati Reds vs. Oakland A's in World Series Game Two, Riverfront Stadium, October 15, 1972**

**BELOW** A sprawling Dick Green of the A's bites the dust at home plate as Reds catcher Johnny Bench follows through after applying a sweep tag. Green was nailed at the plate by left fielder Pete Rose, trying to score from second on a Bert Campaneris single.

**UNTEN** Dick Green von den A's liegt im Staub am Schlagmal, während Reds-Fänger Johnny Bench, der ihn gerade berührt hat, durchzieht. Green war am Mal von Left Fielder Pete Rose erwischt worden, als er versuchte, nach einem Single-Schlag von Bert Campaneris vom zweiten Base aus zu punkten.

**CI-DESSOUS** Dick Green des A's, au sol, mord la poussière en arrivant sur le marbre. Johnny Bench, receveur des Reds, l'accompagne dans sa glissade après l'avoir touché. Green, qui essayait de marquer depuis la deuxième sur un simple de Bert Campaneris, est éliminé grâce au relais du joueur de champ gauche Pete Rose.

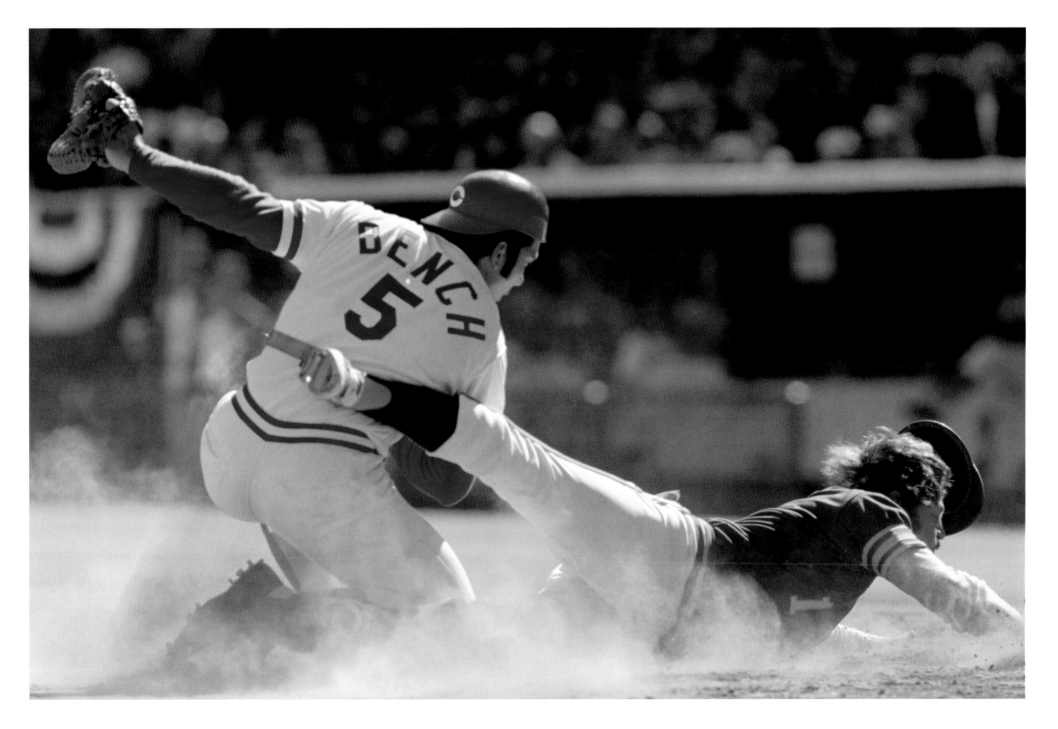

### The decisive moment, New York Yankees vs. Pittsburgh Pirates in World Series Game Seven, Forbes Field, October 13, 1960

**PAGES 238–239** Bill Mazeroski launches the most famous home run in World Series history, a bottom-of-the-ninth blast that gave the Pirates the decisive 10-9 victory and the championship. Umpire Bill Jackowski looks up at the ball's trajectory, while Yankees catcher Johnny Blanchard starts to sink into the ground.

**SEITEN 238–239** Bill Mazeroski startet den berühmtesten Homerun in der Geschichte der World Series, ein gewaltiger Schlag gegen Ende des neunten Innings, der den Pirates den entscheidenden 10:9-Sieg und die Meisterschaft sicherte. Schiedsrichter Bill Jackowski verfolgt die Flugbahn des Balles, während Yankee-Fänger Johnny Blanchard schon zu Boden sinkt.

**PAGES 238–239** Bill Mazeroski expédie le coup de circuit le plus célèbre de l'histoire des World Series à la fin de la neuvième manche. Il offre aux Pirates la victoire 10-9 et le titre. L'arbitre Bill Jackowski observe la trajectoire de la balle. Quant au receveur des Yankees, Johnny Blanchard, il voit la victoire lui échapper.

### Maris holds court, New York Yankees vs. Cincinnati Reds in World Series Game Two, Yankee Stadium, October 5, 1961

**OPPOSITE** Four days after hitting his 61st home run to break Babe Ruth's one-season record, Roger Maris demonstrates his batting stance for a group of photographers and reporters. Most reporters were skeptical about a .269 hitter whose previous high was 39 home runs suddenly holding the most celebrated record in sports.

**GEGENÜBER** Vier Tage, nachdem er seinen 61. Homerun geschlagen und damit den Rekord von Babe Ruth gebrochen hat, demonstriert Roger Maris einer Gruppe von Fotografen und Reportern seinen Schlag. Die meisten Reporter hatten so ihre Zweifel, wie ein .269-Schlagmann, dessen bisherige Höchstleistung bei 39 Homeruns lag, plötzlich den gefeiertsten aller Sportrekorde halten konnte.

**PAGE CI-CONTRE** Quatre jours après avoir frappé son 61ᵉ coup de circuit de la saison et donc avoir battu le record de Babe Ruth, Roger Maris montre sa position à la batte à un groupe de photographes et de journalistes. La plupart d'entre eux restaient encore sceptiques face à ce batteur qui culminait à 0.269, dont le précédent titre de gloire s'établissait à trente-neuf coups de circuit et qui, soudain, décrochait le plus célèbre des records sportifs.

### Maris relaxed, New York Yankees vs. Pittsburgh Pirates in World Series Game Two, Forbes Field, October 6, 1960

**RIGHT** A relaxed Roger Maris flexes his glove on the bench, watching his teammates score 16 runs in a World Series game and not imagining that just one year later, his team's success would be upstaged by his own quest to topple Babe Ruth's hallowed home run record.

**RECHTS** Auf der Bank knetet Roger Maris entspannt seinen Handschuh, während er zusieht, wie sein Team in diesem Spiel der World Series 16 Punkte macht. Er ahnt noch nicht, dass nur ein Jahr später sein Versuch, den geheiligten Homerun-Rekord von Babe Ruth einzustellen, den Erfolg des Teams aus den Schlagzeilen verdrängen wird.

**À DROITE** Roger Maris, détendu, assouplit son gant en observant ses coéquipiers qui marquent seize points dans une partie des World Series. Il ne peut imaginer qu'un an plus tard, le succès des Yankees sera éclipsé par sa propre quête pour battre le record de coups de circuit établi par Babe Ruth.

### Ballet in the dirt, New York Yankees vs. Cincinnati Reds in World Series Game Two, Yankee Stadium, October 5, 1961

**PAGES 246–247** Tony Kubek of the Yankees sprawls after hurtling across the second base bag to prevent Reds shortstop Eddie Kasko from making the throw to first base to complete the double play. Kasko and umpire Augie Donatelli pivot in tandem to watch the play at first as Donatelli signals the out on Kubek.

**SEITEN 246–247** Yankee Tony Kubek liegt ausgestreckt am Boden, nachdem er über das zweite Base geschossen ist, um zu verhindern, dass Eddie Kasko, Shortstop der Reds, den Ball zum ersten Base wirft und so das Double Play vollendet. Kasko und Schiedsrichter Augie Donatelli verfolgen gemeinsam das Spiel am ersten Base, bis Donatelli auf Out gegen Kubek entscheidet.

**PAGES 246–247** Après avoir couru de toutes ses forces, Tony Kubek des Yankees s'écroule sur la deuxième base afin d'empêcher le bloqueur des Reds, Eddie Kasko, de relayer vers la première base et ainsi de parachever le double jeu. Kasko et l'arbitre Augie Donatelli pivotent de conserve pour regarder ce qui se passe en première base. Donatelli signale l'élimination de Kubek.

**"Safe!" Los Angeles Dodgers vs. New York Yankees in World Series Game Five, Dodger Stadium, October 16, 1977**

**BELOW** Steve Garvey, already starting to stand up from his slide into home plate, shouts a gloating "safe!" as Yankees catcher Thurman Munson twists around to apply the tag too late. Garvey scored from second base on a single to give the Dodgers a 7-0 lead in a game they eventually won 10-4.

**UNTEN** Steve Garvey, nach seinem Homerun schon fast wieder auf den Beinen, brüllt triumphierend „Safe!", denn Yankee-Fänger Thurman Munson kommt zu spät, um ihn noch zu berühren. Garvey brachte die Dodgers so nach einem Single-Schlag vom zweiten Base mit 7:0 in Führung; am Ende gewannen sie 10:4.

**CI-DESSOUS** Steve Garvey se relève en jubilant après sa glissade vers le marbre... Il hurle «sauf!» malgré les tentatives tardives de Thurman Munson, le receveur des Yankees, pour le toucher. Garvey a marqué sur un simple en partant de la deuxième base et donne une avance de sept points aux Dodgers qui gagneront finalement 10-4.

**Yaz tees off, Boston Red Sox vs. St. Louis Cardinals in World Series Game Two, Fenway Park, October 5, 1967**

**OPPOSITE** After winning the Triple Crown by leading the American League in batting average, home runs, and runs batted in during the season, Carl Yastrzemski continues his torrid hitting in the World Series by belting a home run, one of two he hit as the Red Sox won 5-0 to even the Series.

**GEGENÜBER** In der American League hatte er bereits die Triple Crown für die beste Schlagstatistik, die meisten Homeruns und RBIs der Saison gewonnen. In der World Series ließ Carl Yastrzemski weitere heiße Schläge wie diesen Homerun folgen, einen von zweien beim 5:0-Sieg, mit dem die Red Sox in der Series gleichzogen.

**PAGE CI-CONTRE** Après avoir gagné la Triple couronne de la Ligue américaine en cumulant la meilleure moyenne, le plus grand nombre de coups de circuit et de points produits, Carl Yastrzemski poursuit son incroyable lancée dans les World Series grâce à deux home runs qui mènent les Red Sox à une victoire 5-0 et leur permettent d'égaliser.

### Yankee Stadium from center field, October 4, 1961

**PAGES 246-247** Nothing matches the majestic sweep and classical façade of Yankee Stadium, viewed from center field as the World Series gets under way. Center field bleacher fans for 18 consecutive years were able to watch immortals Joe DiMaggio or Mickey Mantle patrol the outfield in front of them.

**SEITEN 246-247** Nichts kommt dem majestätischen Schwung und der klassischen Fassade des Yankee-Stadiums gleich – hier der Blick von der Mitte des Feldes bei der Eröffnung der World Series. 18 Jahre konnten die Fans in den Bleachers des Center Field vor sich im Outfield den unsterblichen Joe DiMaggio oder Mickey Mantle beobachten.

**PAGES 246-247** La courbe majestueuse et la façade classique du Yankee Stadium sont incomparables. On les voit ici depuis le champ centre, au cours des World Series. Les spectateurs assis dans ces tribunes ont pu contempler pendant dix-huit années consécutives des immortels tels Joe DiMaggio ou Mickey Mantle qui patrouillaient dans le champ extérieur juste devant eux.

### Koufax vs. Palmer, Los Angeles Dodgers vs. Baltimore Orioles in World Series Game Two, Dodger Stadium, October 6, 1966

**OPPOSITE** Twenty-year-old Orioles ace Jim Palmer takes a big stride toward a Hall of Fame career, polishing off the ninth inning of a World Series shutout. The game also marked the final appearance of fellow Hall of Famer Sandy Koufax, the losing pitcher for the Dodgers, whose swan song was sabotaged by five Dodgers errors and Palmer's gem.

**GEGENÜBER** Jim Palmer, 20-jähriges Ass der Orioles, macht mit einem Shutout im neunten Inning einen großen Schritt in Richtung Hall of Fame. Dieses World-Series-Spiel war auch der letzte Auftritt eines anderen Stars aus der Hall of Fame: Sandy Koufax.

Die Abschiedsvorstellung des Pitchers der Dodgers wurde durch fünf schwere Fehler seiner Mannschaft und Palmers Glanzleistung getrübt.

**PAGE CI-CONTRE** Jim Palmer, lanceur vedette des Orioles, vingt ans. Grâce à un blanchissage en règle lors de la neuvième manche, il fait un bond en avant vers une carrière digne du Temple de la renommée. Cette rencontre marque aussi la dernière apparition d'un autre membre du Temple de la renommée, Sandy Koufax, lanceur malheureux des Dodgers, dont le chant du cygne a été saboté par cinq erreurs de son équipe et par la réussite insolente de Palmer.

### Double play, Los Angeles Dodgers vs. Baltimore Orioles in World Series Game Three, Memorial Stadium, October 8, 1966

**BELOW** Dodgers runner Ron Fairly hardly cares about reaching the base, instead devoting his energy to upending Orioles second baseman Davey Johnson as he makes the pivot on a double-play attempt. The successful double play thwarted a rally in a game where every baserunner was important, a crucial 1-0 victory by the Orioles.

**UNTEN** Dem Dodgers-Runner Ron Fairly geht es nicht darum, das Base zu erreichen, er will Davey Jones, den Second Baseman der Orioles, umhauen, der gerade zu einem Double-Play-Versuch dreht. Das erfolgreiche Double Play verhinderte die Aufholjagd in einem Spiel, in dem jeder Baserunner wichtig war. Am Ende gewannen die Orioles 1:0.

**CI-DESSOUS** Le coureur des Dodgers, Ron Fairly, n'essaie pas vraiment d'atteindre la base. Il consacre toute son énergie à sa tentative pour renverser le deuxième base des Orioles, Davey Johnson, qui lui-même s'efforce de pivoter pour effectuer un double jeu. Le double retrait réussi va contrecarrer la remontée des Dodgers dans une partie où chaque coureur est important. Les Orioles obtiennent une victoire cruciale, 1-0.

**The rundown, New York Yankees vs. San Francisco Giants in World Series Game Two, Candlestick Park, October 5, 1962**

**BELOW** Tom Haller (#5) of the Giants is caught in a rundown after a failed squeeze bunt attempt. All the fielders can get involved in a rundown, as in this case where shortstop Tony Kubek covers third base to receive the throw from first baseman Dale Long and tag Haller out.

**UNTEN** Tom Haller (5) von den Giants ist nach einem fehlgeschlagenen „bunt" zwischen zwei Bases gestrandet und wird nun von allen Feldspielern gejagt. Shortstop Tony Kubek deckt das dritte Base ab, fängt den Ball von First Baseman Dale Long und berührt Haller – out!

**CI-DESSOUS** Tom Haller (n° 5) des Giants est pris dans une souricière après une tentative ratée de jeu risque-tout sur amorti. Tous les joueurs de champ peuvent participer à une souricière: ici on voit le bloqueur Tony Kubeck qui couvre la troisième base afin de recevoir le relais du première base Dale Long et de pouvoir ainsi éliminer Haller sur toucher.

## The run counted, Cincinnati Reds vs Oakland A's in World Series Game One, Riverfront Stadium, October 14, 1972

**BELOW** Everyone looks toward first base on this play, which began with the bases loaded and one out. Trying to turn an inning-ending double play, A's second baseman Dick Green tumbles face-first into the dirt, upended by Reds runner Denis Menke. Johnny Bench crosses the plate with the run that won't count if the double play is completed. The run counted.

**UNTEN** Als dieser Spielzug begann, waren alle Bases besetzt und einer out. Jetzt richteten sich alle Augen aufs erste Base. Bei dem Versuch eines Double Play, mit dem das Inning beendet worden wäre, fällt Dick Green, Second Baseman der A's, mit dem Gesicht in den Dreck, umgehauen von Reds-Läufer Denis Menke. Johnny Bench überquert das Mal mit dem Run, und der Lauf zählte.

**CI-DESSOUS** Tout le monde se tourne vers la première base lors de cette phase de jeu qui a commencé avec quatre bases remplies et une élimination. En essayant de clore la manche sur un double jeu, le deuxième base des A's, Dick Green, s'écroule face contre terre, renversé par le coureur des Reds, Denis Menke. Johnny Bench marque un point en arrivant sur le marbre. L'arbitre va finalement l'accorder.

**Home run, New York Yankees vs. Los Angeles Dodgers in World Series Game Four, Dodger Stadium, October 6, 1963**

**BELOW** Broadcaster Ernie Harwell called it: *"It's a fly ball to deep left, it may be ... it's a home run!"* Mickey Mantle circles the bases after his home run off Koufax, the Yankees' only hurrah in the final game, won by Koufax 2-1. Added broadcaster Joe Garagiola, *"It looked like a high fastball, about letter-high, and he really put a charge into it."*

**UNTEN** Der Rundfunkreporter Ernie Harwell beschrieb es so: *„Es ist ein hoher Ball tief ins linke Feld, es könnte ... es ist ein Homerun!"* Mickey Mantle umkreist die Bases nach seinem Homerun gegen Koufax, aber es ist der einzige Triumph der Yankees im letzten Spiel; Koufax siegt mit 2:1. Joe Garagiolas Kommentar im Radio: *„Es sah aus wie ein schneller, hoher Ball, ungefähr in Brusthöhe, aber er hat ihn wirklich noch erwischt."*

**CI-DESSOUS** Commentaire d'Ernie Harwell: *« C'est une chandelle qui va loin vers la gauche... c'est peut-être... Oui, c'est un home run ! »* Mickey Mantle fait le tour des bases après ce coup de circuit concédé par Koufax, le seul motif de joie des Yankees dans cette ultime partie gagnée par Koufax, 2-1. Le commentateur Joe Garagiola a ajouté: *« Il me semble que c'était une balle rapide haute, à hauteur de poitrine... il l'a vraiment plombée. »*

**On the fence, San Francisco Giants vs. New York Yankees in World Series Game One, Candlestick Park, October 4, 1962**

**OPPOSITE** As spectators rush forward in search of a souvenir, Giants right fielder Felipe Alou makes a desperate leap at a drive hit by Roger Maris in the first inning of the World Series. The ball hit the top of the fence and bounced back on the field, resulting in a double that drove in two runs to help the Yankees win the opener.

**GEGENÜBER** Während Zuschauer auf der Jagd nach einem Souvenir nach vorn drängen, macht Right Fielder Felipe Alou von den Giants im ersten Inning der World Series einen verzweifelten Satz nach einem Schlag von Roger Maris. Der Ball traf den oberen Rand des Zauns und sprang dann ins Feld zurück, was zu einem Double mit zwei Punkten führte und so den Yankees half, das Auftaktspiel zu gewinnen.

**PAGE CI-CONTRE** Alors que les spectateurs se précipitent dans l'espoir de rapporter un souvenir, le champ droit des Giants, Felipe Alou, tente un bond désespéré pour intercepter le coup en flèche de Roger Maris lors de la première manche des World Series. La balle va heurter le sommet de la clôture et rebondir dans le terrain... résultat: un double et deux points marqués par les Yankees qui remporteront ce match d'ouverture.

**Charging home, Baltimore Orioles vs. Cincinnati Reds in World Series Game Three, Memorial Stadium, October 13, 1970**

**BELOW** It's collision time at home plate as Hal McRae of the Reds puts his shoulder into Orioles catcher Andy Etchebarren while trying to score from second on a single. McRae's aggression pays off when the ball drops from Etchebarren's glove. But the Orioles had the last laugh, winning the game 9-3.

**UNTEN** Kollisionszeit am Schlagmal, als Hal McRae von den Reds den Orioles-Fänger Andy Etchebarren mit der Schulter stößt. McRaes Aggression zahlt sich aus, denn

der Ball rutscht aus Etchebarrens Handschuh. Aber am Ende lachten die Orioles und gewannen 9:3.

**CI-DESSOUS** Collision sur le marbre. Hal McRae des Reds donne un coup d'épaule au receveur des Orioles, Andy Etchebarren, dans l'espoir de déloger la balle et de marquer depuis la deuxième base sur un simple. L'agression de McRae va payer: la balle tombe d'Etchebarren gant. Toutefois, les Orioles auront le dernier mot et remporteront la victoire 9-3.

**Shutout, Los Angeles Dodgers vs. New York Yankees in World Series Game Three, Dodger Stadium, October 5, 1963**

**OPPOSITE** Don Drysdale (center) hugs catcher John Roseboro and shakes third baseman Jim Gilliam's hand after tossing a sparkling shutout against the Yankees. The Dodgers scored a run in the first inning, and Drysdale made the slim 1-0 lead stand up the rest of the way, stifling the defending champions on three harmless singles.

**GEGENÜBER** Don Drysdale (M.) um-armt nach einem glänzenden Shut-out gegen die Yankees Fänger John Roseboro und schüttelt Third Baseman Jim Gilliam die Hand. Die Dodgers punkteten im ersten Inning,

und Drysdale sicherte das knappe 1:0 über die Zeit, indem er drei harm-lose Single-Schläge des amtierenden Meisters vereitelte.

**PAGE CI-CONTRE** Don Drysdale (au centre), le bras autour des épaules du receveur John Roseboro, serre la main du troisième base Jim Gilliam après avoir signé un blanchissage contre les Yankees. Les Dodgers ont marqué un point dans la première manche et Drysdale a réussi à conserver ce mai-gre avantage en accordant seulement trois simples inoffensifs aux cham-pions sortants.

**Mel Allen, New York Yankees vs. Cincinnati Reds in World Series Game Five, Crosley Field, October 9, 1961**

**PAGES 256-257** *"How about that!"* crowed legendary Yankees announcer Mel Allen as he interviewed right fielder Johnny Blanchard, whose two home runs and .400 batting average led the Yankees in their five-game drubbing of Cincinnati in the 1961 World Series.

**SEITEN 256-257** „Schau mal einer an!", krähte Mel Allen, der legendäre Stadionsprecher der Yankees, als er Right Fielder Johnny Blanchard interviewte, der die Yankees in Spiel

5 der World Series 1961 mit zwei Homeruns und einer Schlag-Quote von .400 zum Triumph führte.

**PAGES 256-257** « C'est pas génial! » pavoise l'annonceur légendaire des Yankees, Mel Alen, en interrogeant le joueur de champ droit Johnny Blan-chard dont les deux coups de circuit et la moyenne de 0.400 à la batte ont permis aux Yankees d'infliger une raclée à Cincinnati lors des World Series de 1961.

## Up from the minors, New York Yankees vs. Cincinnati Reds in World Series Game One, Yankee Stadium, October 4, 1961

**OPPOSITE** Roger Maris (#9) and Reds first baseman Gordy Coleman reminisce about their early days together in the minor league system of the Cleveland Indians, before trades landed them on pennant-winning teams. Maris, who was hounded by the press during his 1961 chase of Babe Ruth's home run record, is glad to share the spotlight before the start of the World Series.

**GEGENÜBER** Roger Maris (9) und Gordy Coleman, First Baseman der Reds, schwelgen in Erinnerungen an den gemeinsamen Beginn ihrer Karriere in der unteren Spielklasse der Cleveland Indians, bevor sie an Teams verkauft wurden, die den Meistertitel errangen. Maris, der 1961 den Homerun-Rekord von Babe Ruth einstellen wollte und deswegen von der Presse gejagt wurde, freut sich nun, vor Beginn der World Series ebenfalls im Rampenlicht zu stehen.

**PAGE CI-CONTRE** Roger Maris (n° 9) et le première base des Reds, Gordy Coleman, évoquent des souvenirs communs. En ligue mineure, ils jouaient pour les Cleveland Indians, avant d'être transférés dans le haut du panier. Maris, harcelé par la presse en 1961 lors de sa poursuite du record de coups de circuit de Babe Ruth, est ravi de pouvoir partager les feux de la rampe avant le début des World Series.

## Houk at the helm, New York Yankees vs. Cincinnati Reds in World Series Game Four, Crosley Field, October 8, 1961

**PAGES 260-261** Talking through his customary chew of tobacco, Yankees manager Ralph Houk tells reporters how he expects his team to polish off the Reds in two more games. That's exactly what they did, trouncing the Reds 7-0 and 13-5 to give Houk a championship in his first year at the helm.

**SEITEN 260-261** Den Mund wie immer voller Kautabak, erklärt Yankee-Trainer Ralph Houk Reportern, dass er mit seinem Team die Reds in den nächsten beiden Spielen vom Platz fegen werde. Und genau das taten sie: Sie schlugen die Reds mit 7:0 und 13:5, und Houk gewann in seinem ersten Jahr als Trainer die Meisterschaft.

**PAGES 260-261** Le manager des Yankees, Ralph Houk, la joue gonflée par sa traditionnelle chique. Houk explique aux journalistes pourquoi il pense que ses joueurs vont encore mettre une raclée aux Reds dans les deux dernières parties. L'avenir lui donne raison avec des résultats de 7-0 et 13-5 pour les Reds. Houk remporte le championnat pour sa première année à la barre.

## Ted Williams, Forbes Field, October 6, 1960

**BELOW** Just one week after retiring as a player, Ted Williams takes in the action as part of a special assignment on the World Series for *Life* magazine. It was an ironic role for a player who spent his career battling what he called *"the ink-stained wretches of the Boston press."*

**UNTEN** Nur eine Woche nach seinem Rücktritt als aktiver Spieler ist Ted Williams schon wieder bei der World Series dabei – als Sonderkorrespondent der Illustrierten *Life*. Es war eine merkwürdige Aufgabe für einen Spieler, der seine Karriere damit verbracht hatte, sich mit der Presse in Boston anzulegen.

**CI-DESSOUS** Une semaine seulement après avoir pris sa retraite de joueur, Ted Williams retrouve les World Series en tant que reporter pour le magazine *Life*. Plutôt ironique pour un joueur qui a passé toute sa carrière à combattre la presse de Boston.

## Lonborg at work, Boston Red Sox vs. St. Louis Cardinals in World Series, Fenway Park, 1967

**LEFT** Red Sox ace Jim Lonborg, who came of age in 1967 by winning 22 games, stood tall in the World Series as well. He tossed a one-hitter against the Cardinals in his Series debut and stifled them with a three-hitter in Game Five—coming within one out of another shutout before Roger Maris homered in the ninth inning—before being outgunned by Bob Gibson in Game Seven.

**LINKS** Jim Lonborg von den Red Sox wurde 1967 mit 22 gewonnenen Spielen zum Star und zeichnete sich auch in der World Series aus. In seinem Debüt gegen die Cardinals ließ er nur einen Hit zu und schaltete sie auch in Spiel 5 aus, als er nur drei Hits erlaubte, wobei er im neunten Inning nur einen Schlag vor einem weiteren Shutout stand, dann aber einen Homerun von Roger Maris zulassen musste. In Spiel 7 musste er sich allerdings Bob Gibson beugen.

**A GAUCHE** Meilleur lanceur des Red Sox, Jim Lonborg, arrive à maturité en 1967 en remportant vingt-deux parties. Il tient aussi son rang lors des World Series. Pour ses débuts, il n'accorde qu'un seul coup sûr aux Cardinals, puis trois dans la cinquième partie (dans la neuvième manche, il n'est plus qu'à un retrait du blanchissage lorsque Roger Maris frappe un coup de circuit). Il est alors surpassé par Bob Gibson dans la septième.

## Lonborg at rest, Boston Red Sox vs. St. Louis Cardinals in World Series Game Five, Busch Stadium, October 9, 1967

**OPPOSITE** Soaking his arm in icy water to reduce the swelling that comes with pitching nine innings of baseball, Jim Lonborg tells reporters how he muffled the potent Cardinals lineup for the second time in two starts.

**GEGENÜBER** Pitcher Jim Lonborg taucht seinen nach neun Innings geschwollenen Wurfarm in Eiswasser und erzählt Reportern, wie er die mächtigen Schlagmänner der Cardinals zum zweiten Mal hintereinander in Schach gehalten hat.

**PAGE CI-CONTRE** Jim Lonborg, après avoir lancé durant neuf manches de baseball, trempe son bras dans l'eau glacée pour le soulager. Lonborg explique aux journalistes comment il a étouffé les ardeurs de la puissante équipe de départ des Cardinals pour la seconde fois en tant que premier lanceur.

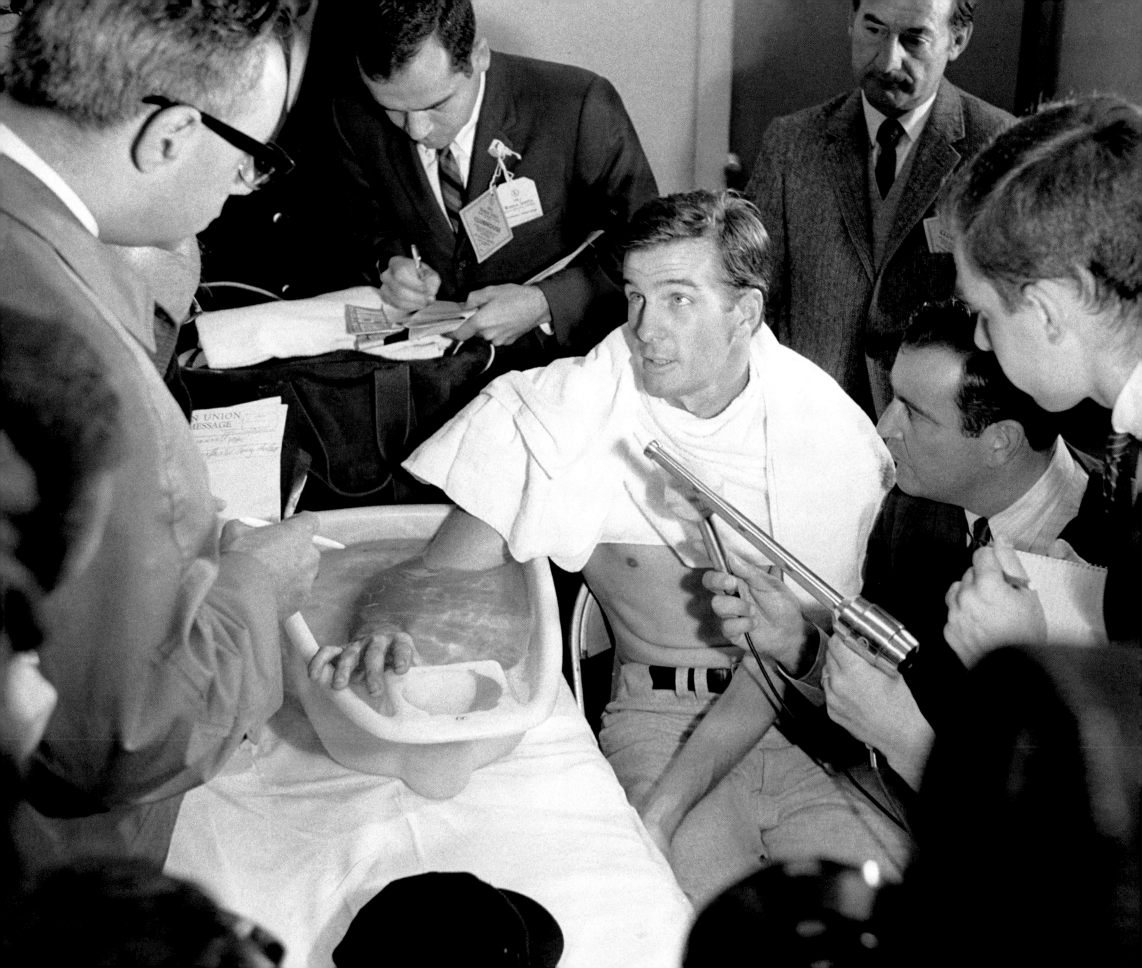

**Out at second, New York Yankees vs. Pittsburgh Pirates in World Series Game Two, Forbes Field, October 6, 1960**

**BELOW** Dick Groat of the Pirates, having failed to prevent the throw by second baseman Bobby Richardson, turns to see whether the double play has been completed at first base. The batter was safe at first but it didn't matter much as the Yankees pounded out 19 hits, including two home runs by Mickey Mantle, to trounce the Pirates 16-3.

**UNTEN** Nachdem er den Wurf von Second Baseman Bobby Richardson nicht verhindern konnte, schaut Dick Groat von den Pirates nach oben, um zu sehen, ob es mit dem Double Play am ersten Base geklappt hat. Der Schlagmann schaffte es sicher zum ersten Base, aber die Yankees erzielten 19 Treffer, darunter zwei Homeruns von Mickey Mantle, und vernichteten die Pirates mit 16:3.

**CI-DESSOUS** Dick Groat des Pirates, qui n'a pas réussi à empêcher le relais du deuxième base Bobby Richardson, se retourne pour voir si le double jeu a réussi en première base. Victoire, le batteur est sauf en première. Les Yankees ont frappé dix-neuf coups sûrs dans cette partie, dont deux coups de circuit réalisés par Mickey Mantle. Ils écraseront les Pirates 16-3.

**Out at third, Los Angeles Dodgers vs. Minnesota Twins in World Series Game Five, Dodger Stadium, October 11, 1965**

**Tiebreaker, New York Yankees vs. Cincinnati Reds in World Series Game Three, Crosley Field, October 7, 1961**

**BELOW** The 1965 Dodgers featured two great base stealers: Maury Wills, the first man to steal 100 bases in a season, and Willie Davis, who tied a World Series record in this game with three steals. Then there is the diving Dick Tracewski, who will be out by a mile when third baseman Harmon Killebrew catches the quick throw from catcher Earl Battey.

**UNTEN** 1965 hatten die Dodgers zwei Asse, die sich darauf verstanden, ein Base zu stehlen: Maury Wills und Willie Davis. Und dann ist da noch Dick Tracewski, dieser Sprinter, der schon meilenweit entfernt ist, als Third Baseman Harmon Killebrew den schnellen Wurf von Fänger Earl Battey fängt.

**CI-DESSOUS** L'équipe de 1965 des Dodgers comptait deux grands voleurs de bases: Maury Wills et Willie Davis. Mais il y avait aussi Dick Tracewski, en plein plongeon, sur cette photographie. Il sera encore bien loin du but que le troisième base Harmon Killebrew aura déjà attrapé le relais rapide du receveur Earl Battey.

**PAGES 266–267** Fresh from breaking Babe Ruth's record with 61 home runs during the season, Roger Maris adds World Series heroics, blasting a ninth-inning home run to break a 2-2 tie. The game-winning hit put the Yankees ahead two games to one and broke the Reds' backs, as the Yankees romped in the final two games to take the title.

**SEITEN 266–267** Gerade hatte er mit 61 Homeruns in einer Saison den Rekord von Babe Ruth gebrochen, da wurde Roger Maris auch noch zum World-Series-Helden, als er im neunten Inning mit einem explosiven Homerun den entscheidenden Punkt zum 3:2 erzielte. Die Yankees lagen nun in Führung, hatten den Widerstand der Reds gebrochen und holten sich mit zwei weiteren Siegen den Titel.

**PAGES 266–267** Maris vient de battre le record de soixante et un coups de circuit frappés dans une saison établi par Babe Ruth, lorsqu'il ajoute les World Series à son palmarès. Les deux équipes sont à égalité (2-2) dans la neuvième manche quand il expédie un formidable coup de circuit et donne l'avantage aux Yankees. Les Yankees gagneront facilement les deux dernières parties et remporteront le titre.

**Pop-up, Baltimore Orioles vs. Los Angeles Dodgers in World Series Game One, Dodger Stadium, October 5, 1966**

**PAGES 268-269** Dodgers shortstop Maury Wills gazes up into the sky, his sunglasses flipped down to deflect the sun's glare, and spreads his arms wide to signal teammates that he won't need any help corralling the pop-up.

**SEITEN 268-269** Durch die Sonnenbrille geschützt, starrt Dodgers-Shortstop Maury Wills in den Himmel und breitet die Arme aus, um seinen Teamkameraden anzuzeigen, dass er keine Unterstützung braucht, um den hohen Ball zu fangen.

**PAGES 268-269** Le bloqueur des Dodgers, Maury Wills, observe le ciel derrière ses lunettes de soleil. Il tend les bras pour signaler à ses coéquipiers qu'il n'aura pas besoin d'aide pour intercepter cette petite chandelle.

**Oakland A's vs. New York Mets in World Series Game Six, Oakland-Alameda County Coliseum, October 20, 1973**

**BELOW** Displaying the balance and leverage of perfect power swing, Reggie Jackson of the A's belts one of two run-scoring doubles that helped the A's win 3-1 and send the Series to a seventh game. This was an early instance of World Series heroics that resulted in Jackson being dubbed "Mr. October."

**UNTEN** Jerry Grote, der Fänger der Mets, kann es nicht mit ansehen, wie Reggie Jackson von den A's einen der zwei erfolgreichen Doubles schlägt, die zum 3:1-Sieg der A's beitrugen und ein siebtes Spiel erforderlich machten. Dies war eine der frühen Heldentaten in den World Series und trug Jackson den Spitznamen „Mr. October" ein.

**CI-DESSOUS** Le receveur des Mets, Jerry Grote, préfère ne pas voir Reggie Jackson des A's frapper un double. L'un des deux doubles à deux points qu'il marquera pour faire gagner les A's 3 à 1 et les envoyer dans une septième partie. C'est l'un des nombreux exploits en World Series qui feront attribuer à Jackson, le surnom de «Monsieur Octobre».

**Standing guard, Boston Red Sox vs. St. Louis Cardinals in World Series Game Two, Fenway Park, October 5, 1967**

**OPPOSITE** A mounted policeman stands guard at one of the greatest pitching performances in Series history. Jim Lonborg retired the first 19 Cardinals he faced and still had a no-hitter with two outs in the eighth inning when Julian Javier doubled. It was only the fourth World Series one-hitter.

**GEGENÜBER** Ein berittener Polizist hält Wache bei einer der größten Pitcher-Vorstellungen in der Geschichte der Series. Jim Lonborg erlaubte den ersten 19 Schlagmännern der Cardinals keinen Punkt, hatte auch im achten Inning noch keinen Punkt zugelassen und zwei Cardinals ins Out geschickt, als Julian Javier ein Double gelang – der einzige Punkt, den Lonborg erlaubte.

**PAGE CI-CONTRE** La police montée surveille l'une des plus grandes performances au lancer de toute l'histoire des World Series. Jim Lonborg a éliminé les dix-neuf premiers Cardinals qu'il a affrontés. Il n'a toujours concédé aucun coup sûr à ses adversaires dans la huitième manche, lorsque, Julian Javier marque un double.

**"Boog" connects, Los Angeles Dodgers vs. Baltimore Orioles in World Series Game One, Dodger Stadium, October 5, 1966**

**OPPOSITE** Dodgers catcher John Roseboro and umpire Bill Jackowski peer around the bulky John "Boog" Powell to watch the line drive he has just hit to right field. Note that nearly every man in the crowd is wearing a white shirt and a tie, a long-standing tradition that disappeared when World Series games began being played at night in the 1970s.

**GEGENÜBER** Dodgers-Fänger John Roseboro und Schiedsrichter Bill Jackowski spähen an dem massigen John „Boog" Powell vorbei, um den flachen Line Drive zu verfolgen, den der gerade ins rechte Feld geschlagen hat. Man beachte, dass fast alle männlichen Zuschauer ein weißes Hemd und eine Krawatte tragen, eine langjährige Tradition, die erst endete, als in den 1970ern die ersten Spiele der World Series abends stattfanden.

**PAGE CI-CONTRE** Le receveur des Dodgers, John Roseboro, et l'arbitre Bill Jackowski observent le coup en flèche frappé vers le champ droit par le massif John « Boog » Powell. On note que la plupart des hommes présents dans le public portent une chemise blanche et une cravate, une vieille tradition disparue dans les années soixante-dix lorsque les rencontres du World Series sont devenues nocturnes.

**Like a great bird, Los Angeles Dodgers vs. Minnesota Twins in World Series Game One, Metropolitan Stadium, October 6, 1965**

**BELOW** Don Drysdale's arm reaches its full extension before whipping around in the sidearm delivery that intimidated National League hitters for a dozen years. The scowling six-foot-five workhorse disdained hitters and relished his reputation as the leading proponent of the "knockdown" pitch thrown at the batter's head.

**UNTEN** Don Drysdale streckt seinen Arm so weit wie möglich aus, um Schwung für den Wurf zu nehmen, fast, als wolle er mit einer Waffe zustechen. Mit dieser Wurftechnik lehrte er die Schlagmänner ein Dutzend Jahre lang das Fürchten.

Drysdale, ein mürrisches, über 1,95 m großes Arbeitstier, verachtete die Schlagmänner und genoss seinen Ruf als K.-o.-Pitcher, der auf den Kopf des Schlagmanns zielte.

**CI-DESSOUS** Le bras de Don Drysdale atteint son extension maximale avant de fouetter l'air d'un lancer de côté qui impressionne les batteurs de la Ligue nationale depuis une douzaine d'années. Le colosse d'un mètre quatre-vingt-quinze méprisait les frappeurs et savourait sa réputation de partisan en chef des balles dangereuses lancées au ras de la tête.

## Los Angeles Dodgers vs. Minnesota Twins in World Series Game Five, Dodger Stadium, October 11, 1965

**LEFT** Sandy Koufax's elegant pitching motion reveals the tremendous effort behind every pitch he threw. After tossing a sparkling four-hit shutout to put the Dodgers ahead in the Series, Koufax told broadcaster Vin Scully, *"I feel like I'm a hundred years old."* Nevertheless, he pitched another shutout in Game Seven despite only two days' rest for his arthritic elbow.

**LINKS** Sandy Koufax' elegante Bewegung beim Pitchen zeigt die gewaltige Anstrengung, die er in jeden Wurf hineinlegte. Nachdem er die Dodgers mit einem glänzenden Shutout bei nur vier Hits in der Series in Führung gebracht hatte, sagte er dem Reporter Vin Scully: *„Ich komm' mir vor, als sei ich hundert Jahre alt."* Und trotzdem gelang ihm in Spiel 7 ein weiterer Shutout – obwohl er seinem arthritischen Ellbogen nur zwei Ruhetage gönnen konnte.

**A GAUCHE** On perçoit derrière l'élégance du mouvement de Sandy Koufax l'effort incroyable qu'il déploie à chaque lancer. Après avoir concédé seulement quatre coups sûrs lors d'un blanchissage étonnant et placé les Dodgers en tête dans les World Series, Koufax a avoué au commentateur Vin Scully *« J'ai l'impression d'avoir cent ans. »* Néanmoins, il obtiendra un nouveau blanchissage à la septième partie malgré les deux petits jours de repos accordés à son coude atteint d'arthrite.

## Celebration, Los Angeles Dodgers vs. New York Yankees in World Series Game Four, Dodger Stadium, October 6, 1963

**OPPOSITE** The normally placid Sandy Koufax erupts with joy as teammates Maury Wills (#30) and Johnny Roseboro rush to congratulate him after he completed the Dodgers' four-game sweep of the Yankees. Koufax tossed a pair of six-hitters and struck out 23 Yankees, defeating Whitey Ford twice.

**GEGENÜBER** Der sonst so ruhige Sandy Koufax explodiert vor Freude, als ihm seine Mannschaftskameraden Maury Wills (30) und Johnny Roseboro nach dem glatten 4:0-Triumph über die Yankees gratulieren. Koufax warf zwei Spiele mit nur sechs gegnerischen Treffern, erlaubte 23 Yankees keinen einzigen Treffer und siegte zweimal gegen Whitey Ford.

**PAGE CI-CONTRE** Sandy Koufax, généralement placide, saute de joie au moment où ses coéquipiers, Maury Wills (n° 30) et Johnny Roseboro, se précipitent pour le féliciter. Il vient pour la quatrième fois de balayer les Yankees en ne concédant, à deux reprises, que six coups sûrs, en éliminant vingt-trois adversaires et en battant Whitey Ford à deux occasions.

2 3 4 5 6 7 8 9 10 R H E
000000002 2 4 3 AT BAT 12 POS. 3B
00000030 3 5 1 BALL 2 STRIKE 1
OUT 3

**New York Yankees vs. San Francisco Giants in World Series Game Three, Yankee Stadium, October 7, 1962**

**OPPOSITE** As the bullpen pitchers dash across the field to the clubhouse, Yankees pitcher Bill Stafford pats catcher Elston Howard on the back following their narrow escape in the ninth inning. As the scoreboard shows, the Yankees almost squandered a 3-0 lead in the ninth inning.

**GEGENÜBER** Während die Einwechsel-Pitcher über das Feld zum Clubhaus eilen, klopft Pitcher Bill Stafford Fänger Elston Howard auf den Rücken, nachdem sie im neunten Inning gerade noch einmal davon gekommen sind. Wie die Anzeige-tafel zeigt, verspielten die Yankees im neunten Inning beinahe eine 3:0-Führung.

**PAGE CI-CONTRE** Les lanceurs de relève traversent le terrain en direction des vestiaires. Le lanceur des Yankees, Bill Stafford félicite son coéquipier, le receveur Elston Howard, en lui tapant dans le dos. Ils ont réussi à se tirer d'un mauvais pas dans la neuvième manche. Comme l'indique le tableau d'affichage, les Yankees ont presque gâché leur avance 3-0 dans la neuvième.

**Casey leads his troops, New York Yankees vs. Pittsburgh Pirates in World Series Game Two, Forbes Field, October 6, 1960**

**BELOW** A determined Casey Stengel leads catcher Elston Howard and other Yankees to the clubhouse following their 16-3 romp in Game Two. A week later, the 70-year-old manager's 12-year tenure with the Yankees ended in disaster when the Pirates won the championship in their final turn at bat.

**UNTEN** Ein entschlossener Casey Stengel führt Fänger Elston Howard und andere Yankees nach ihrem klaren 16:3 in Spiel 2 zum Clubhaus. Eine Woche später endete die 12-jährige Amtszeit des 70-Jährigen mit einer Katastrophe, als die Pirates mit ihrem letzten Schlagmann die Meisterschaft gewannen.

**CI-DESSOUS** Casey Stengel, résolu, guide le receveur Elston Howard et quelques-uns de ses coéquipiers vers les vestiaires après leur victoire 16 à 3 dans la deuxième rencontre. Une semaine plus tard, le mandat de douze ans du manager septuagénaire des Yankees va se conclure sur un désastre: les Pirates gagnent le championnat dans leur dernier tour de batte.

**Four-game sweep, Los Angeles Dodgers vs. New York Yankees in World Series Game Four, Dodger Stadium, October 6, 1963**

**OPPOSITE** Interviewing winning pitcher Sandy Koufax in the clubhouse while the Dodgers begin to celebrate their championship, broadcaster Vin Scully puts the event in perspective: *"Dodger Stadium is two years old, and the Dodgers have done something that has never been done before. They've swept the Yankees in the World Series."*

**GEGENÜBER** Während die Siegesfeier der Dodgers beginnt, interviewt Rundfunkreporter Vin Scully den siegreichen Pitcher Sandy Koufax und gibt dem Ereignis die richtige Bedeutung: *„Das Dodger Stadium ist zwei Jahre alt, und die Dodgers haben etwas vollbracht, was es vorher noch nie gegeben hat. Sie haben die World Series glatt mit 4:0 gegen die Yankees gewonnen."*

**PAGE CI-CONTRE** Tandis que les Dodgers commencent à fêter leur titre, le commentateur Vin Scully s'entretient avec le lanceur Sandy Koufax dans les vestiaires. Il met leur victoire en perspective : « *Le Dodger Stadium n'a que deux ans d'existence. Les Dodgers ont fait ce qu'aucune équipe n'avait jamais réussi à faire. Ils ont balayé les Yankees dans les World Series.* »

**Champagne bath, Baltimore Orioles vs. Cincinnati Reds in World Series Game Five, Memorial Stadium, October 15, 1970**

**BELOW** Orioles catcher Elrod Hendricks celebrates winning the World Series in the fashion that has been the custom since the 1950s: getting champagne poured over his head by frenzied teammates. Hendricks was a fixture on the Orioles for more than three decades as a player and a coach.

**UNTEN** Orioles-Fänger Elrod Hendricks feiert den Sieg in der World Series so, wie es seit den 1950ern Brauch ist: Er lässt sich von seinen jubelnden Mannschaftskameraden Champagner über den Kopf gießen. Hendricks gehörte als Spieler und als Trainer mehr als drei Jahrzehnte lang zum Inventar der Orioles.

**CI-DESSOUS** Le receveur des Orioles, Elrod Hendricks, célèbre la victoire de son équipe dans les Worlds Series selon la tradition établie depuis les années 1950: des coéquipiers surexcités lui ont versé du champagne sur la tête. Hendricks restera indéboulonnable chez les Orioles pendant plus de trois décennies, d'abord en tant que joueur puis comme entraîneur.

### The underdogs celebrate, New York Yankees vs. Pittsburgh Pirates in World Series Game Seven, Forbes Field, October 13, 1960

**PAGES 280-281** Reporters surround jubilant members of the Pittsburgh Pirates after their shocking World Series triumph over the heavily favored New York Yankees. The players whooping it up in the center of the throng are Don Hoak (right), Dick Schofield (left), and Roy Face (#26).

**SEITEN 280-281** Reporter umringen die jubelnden Spieler der Pittsburgh Pirates nach ihrem völlig überraschenden Triumph über die hoch favorisierten Yankees. Die Spieler – in der Mitte der Meute Don Hoak (r.), Dick Schofield (l.) und Roy Face (26) – lassen die Sau raus.

**PAGES 280-281** Les journalistes se pressent autour des Pittsburgh Pirates après leur victoire triomphale – et surprenante – contre les New York Yankees, donnés pourtant largement favoris. Les joueurs Don Hoak (à droite), Dick Schofield (à gauche) et Roy Face (n° 26) fêtent leur succès.

### Champagne flows, St. Louis Cardinals vs. Boston Red Sox, World Series Game Seven, Fenway Park, October 12, 1967

**LEFT** Every member of the 25-man roster is vital on a championship team and celebrates with equal ecstasy. Phil Gagliano (left), a reserve infielder who had only one turn at bat in the 1967 World Series, pours champagne on star third baseman Mike Shannon, whose home run was the key hit in Game Three.

**LINKS** Jeder Spieler aus dem 25 Mann starken Kader ist von Bedeutung für das Team das Meisters und feiert mit derselben Begeisterung. Phil Gagliano (l.), ein Reserve-Infielder, der 1967 nur einmal als Schlagmann zum Zuge kam, begießt Third Baseman Mike Shannon, den Star, dessen Homerun der Schlüssel für den Sieg in Spiel 3 war, mit Champagner.

**À GAUCHE** Chaque membre de l'effectif de vingt-cinq hommes est vital pour l'équipe lors d'un championnat et célèbre la victoire avec le même bonheur. Phil Gagliano (à gauche), joueur de champ remplaçant n'a connu qu'un seul tour de batte lors des World Series de 1967. On le voit verser du champagne sur le troisième base vedette, Mike Shannon, dont le coup de circuit de la troisième partie a été la clé du succès.

**The A's celebrate, Cincinnati Reds vs. Oakland A's in World Series Game Seven, Riverfront Stadium, October 22, 1972**

**"Walking on the moon," New York Mets vs. Baltimore Orioles in World Series Game Five, Shea Stadium, October 16, 1969**

**BELOW** Oakland players converge in the middle of the field to celebrate the final out of their clinching victory over Cincinnati by piling onto each other. In the center of the pack, without a cap, is manager Dick Williams.

**UNTEN** Spieler der Oakland A's laufen in die Mitte des Spielfelds, fallen sich in die Arme und feiern das letzte Out bei ihrem entscheidenden Sieg über Cincinnati. In der Mitte der Traube, ohne Kappe: Trainer Dick Williams.

**CI-DESSOUS** Les joueurs d'Oakland convergent vers le milieu du terrain pour fêter la dernière élimination de leur écrasante victoire sur Cincinnati. Au centre du rassemblement de joueurs, sans casquette, le manager Dick Williams

**PAGES 284-285** The Mets were perennial doormats whose fans joked, *"The Mets will win a pennant—when a man walks on the moon..."* Less than three months after Neil Armstrong's historic lunar footstep, the "Amazin' Mets" were champions, and their frenzied fans trampled the field.

**SEITEN 284-285** Die Mets waren stets nur Kanonenfutter und ihre Fans witzelten gerne: *„Die Mets werden erst dann Meister, wenn ein Mensch auf dem Mond gelandet ist ..."* Weniger als drei Monate nach Neil Armstrongs historischem ersten Schritt auf dem Mond waren die „fantastischen Mets" Meister und ihre jubelnden Fans stürmten das Spielfeld.

**PAGES 284-285** Les fans des Mets se moquaient gentiment de leur équipe de perdants préférée : « *Les Mets gagneront le titre... quand l'homme marchera sur la lune...* » Moins de trois mois après le premier pas historique de Neil Armstrong sur notre satellite, les « Amazin » Mets devenaient champions et leurs admirateurs transis envahissaient le terrain.

283

"You spend a good piece of your life gripping a baseball, and in the end it turns out that it was the other way around all the time."

—*Jim Bouton*, BALL FOUR, 1970

**Roger Angell, The Summer Game:**

**OPPOSITE** *"I had no answer for the question posed by that youngster in the infield who held up—amid the crazily leaping crowds, the showers of noise and paper, the vermilion smoke-comb clouds, and the vanishing lawns—a sign that said 'WHAT NEXT?' What was past was good enough."*

**GEGENÜBER** *„Ich wusste keine Antwort für diesen jungen Mann im Innenfeld, der – mitten in der wie verrückt hüpfenden Menge, dem Schauer von Lärm und Papier und unter rötlichen Rauchwolken über den langsam verschwindenden Grün des Rasens – ein Schild hochhielt mit der Frage: ‚UND WAS KOMMT ALS NÄCHSTES?' Was geschehen war, war schließlich gut genug."*

**PAGE CI-CONTRE** « *Je n'ai pas la réponse à la question posée par ce jeune admirateur sur le terrain qui tient à bout de bras – au milieu d'une foule qui saute de joie, au milieu du bruit et des confettis, des nuages de fumée vermillon, d'une pelouse qui a disparu – qui tient, donc, une pancarte où l'on peut lire « WHAT NEXT ? » [Jusqu'où iront-ils ?] Je n'ai pas de réponse, car ce qui venait d'arriver me suffisait amplement.* »

# NEIL LEIFER: LIFE AND WORK

By 1960, at age 17, Neil Leifer had his first pictures published in *Sports Illustrated* and he was on his way: He went on to create over 200 covers for *SI*, *Time*, and *People*. Photographed 15 Olympic Games, 4 World Soccer Cups, 17 Kentucky Derbies, 15 Masters golf tournaments, countless World Series, the first 12 Super Bowls, and every major heavyweight championship title boxing match since Floyd Patterson fought Ingemar Johansson in 1960. In addition, he photographed Muhammad Ali's entire career. Today, he produces and directs films, while still doing the occasional photo shoot.

## CHRONOLOGY

**1942**  Born to Betty and Abraham Leifer. Raised in the Vladick Housing Project on the Lower East Side of Manhattan.

**1948**  Brother Howie born.

**1952**  Joins Henry Street Settlement Photo Club. Meets Johnny Iacono. The two become sports photographers and lifelong friends.

**1956**  Delivers sandwiches for his Uncle Sam at the Stage Delicatessen in midtown Manhattan. Often gets tipped in film when he delivers to nearby *Life* photo studio.

**1957**  Attends Seward Park high school. Becomes picture editor of *The Seward World* school paper.

**1958**  On his 16th birthday, gains admission to the NFL title football game between the New York Giants and the Baltimore Colts by wheeling in disabled Army veterans. Takes one of his best-known photos, Alan Ameche's game-winning "Sudden Death" touchdown.

**1961**  First cover of *Sports Illustrated*, New York Giants quarterback Y. A. Tittle.

**1965**  Takes his best-known photograph, a glaring Muhammad Ali towering over a knocked-out Sonny Liston. Marries Renae.

**1967**  Daughter Jodi born.

**1971**  Son Corey born.

**1972**  Becomes a staff photographer for *Sports Illustrated*.

**1978**  Leaves *Sports Illustrated* to become a staff photographer for *Time*.

**1979**  Directs first feature film, *Yesterday's Hero*.

**1988**  While on staff at *Time*, becomes contributing photographer at *Life*.

**1990**  Leaves Time, Inc. to join friend and editor-in-chief Frank Deford as director of photography for *The National* .

**1991**  During the Gulf War, became *Life* magazine's chief of photographic operations in Saudia Arabia.

**1996**  Grandson Joey born.

**1998**  Granddaughter Taylor born.

**2002**  Meets fiancée Randye Beth Stein.

**2006**  Granddaughter Riley born. Awarded the Lucie Award for photographic "Achievement in Sports."

## SELECTED BIBLIOGRAPHY

*Sports. A Collection of Leifer Sports Photographs*. Abrams, 1978.

*Neil Leifer's Sports Stars*. Doubleday, 1985.

*Muhammad Ali: Memories*. Rizzoli, 1992.

*Safari*. Reader's Digest, 1992.

*Sports*. Collins, 1992.

*The Best of Leifer*. Abbeville Press, 2001.

*Neil Leifer: Portraits*. St. Ann's Press, 2003.

*GOAT: A Tribute to Muhammad Ali*. TASCHEN, 2004. One of two principal photographers.

*A Year in Sports*. Abbeville Press, 2006.

## FILMOGRAPHY

*Yesterday's Hero*, 1979. Director. Feature film starring Suzanne Somers and Ian McShane.

*Trading Hearts*, 1987. Director. Feature film starring Raul Julia and Beverly D'Angelo.

*Rosebud*, 1991. Producer, director. Short film.

*The Great White Hype*, 1992. Director. Short film starring Bill Murray.

*Scout's Honor*, 1999. Producer, director. Short film starring Alec Baldwin and Bill Murray.

*Picture Perfect*, 2001. Co-producer. HBO documentary on the iconic sports photographs of our time.

*Smallroom Dancing*, 2002. Producer, director. Short film.

*The Best of Leifer*, 2002. Co-producer, subject. Two-hour ESPN documentary based on his 2001 book. Received an Emmy nomination for "Outstanding Sports Documentary."

*Steamed Dumplings*, 2003. Producer, writer, director. Short film.

*You Write Better than You Play: The Frank Deford Story*, 2004. Producer, director. 90-minute ESPN documentary. Received an Emmy nomination for "Outstanding Sports Documentary."

*God's Gift*, 2006. Producer, writer, director. Short film.

*Portraits of a Lady*, 2007. Director, co-producer. 40-minute HBO documentary.

### Shea Stadium, New York, 1967

**OPPOSITE** Like a flying saucer hovering over the Manhattan skyline, Shea Stadium—one of the generation of cookie-cutter stadiums built in the 1960s to showcase both baseball and football—hosts a Mets game.

**GEGENÜBER** Wie eine Fliegende Untertasse hängt das Shea Stadium – hier während eines Spiels der Mets – über der Skyline von Manhattan, einer jener in den Sechzigern in Serie gebauten Schaukästen für Baseball- und Football-Spiele.

**PAGE CI-CONTRE** Comme une soucoupe volante planant au-dessus de Manhattan, le Shea Stadium est l'un de ces stades en forme de moule à gâteaux qui ont été bâtis dans les années soixante, capables d'accueillir à la fois du baseball et du football américain. On voit ici une partie des Mets.

# NEIL LEIFER: LEBEN UND WERK

Neil Leifer war gerade 17, als 1960 seine ersten Fotos in der Zeitschrift *Sports Illustrated (SI)* veröffentlicht wurden – und damit fing alles an: Fortan lieferte er über 200 Titelbilder für *SI*, *Time* und *People*, fotografierte 15 Olympische Spiele, 4 Fußball-Weltmeisterschaften, 17 Kentucky-Derbys, 15 Masters-Golfturniere, ungezählte World Series, die ersten 12 Super Bowls sowie jeden wichtigen Kampf um die Weltmeisterschaft im Schwergewichtsboxen seit der Begegnung 1960 zwischen Floyd Patterson und Ingemar Johansson. Außerdem begleitete er, den Finger immer am Auslöser, Muhammad Alis gesamte Karriere. Heute ist er als Filmregisseur und -produzent tätig, nimmt aber gelegentlich auch noch mal die Kamera zur Hand.

## CHRONOLOGIE

**1942**  Als Sohn von Betty und Abraham Leifer geboren. Aufgewachsen im Vladick-Komplex, einer Anlage des sozialen Wohnungsbaus an der Lower East Side von Manhattan.

**1948**  Bruder Howie wird geboren.

**1952**  Wird Mitglied im Henry Street Settlement Photo Club. Trifft dort Johnny Iacona, der ebenfalls Sportfotograf wird und mit dem ihn eine lebenslange Freundschaft verbindet.

**1956**  Liefert für seinen Onkel Sam und dessen „Stage Delicatessen" in Midtown Manhattan Sandwiches aus. Bei Lieferungen ins nahe gelegene *Life*-Fotostudio lässt er sich häufig Filme als Trinkgeld geben.

**1957**  Einschulung in die Seward Park High School. Wird Bildredakteur der Schülerzeitung *The Seward World*.

**1958**  An seinem 16. Geburtstag schiebt er behinderte ehemalige Kriegsteilnehmer mit ihren Rollstühlen ins Stadion und erhält so freien Eintritt zum Titelkampf der NFL zwischen den New York Giants und den Baltimore Colts. Schießt eines seiner bekanntesten Fotos: den entscheidenden Touchdown von Alan Ameche in der Verlängerung.

**1961**  Erstes Titelbild in *Sports Illustrated*: Quarterback Y. A. Tittle von den New York Giants.

**1965**  Schießt sein berühmtes Foto, auf dem  Muhammad Ali mit stechendem Blick auf den gerade k. o. geschlagenen Sonny Liston hinabschaut. Heiratet Renae.

**1967**  Tochter Jodi wird geboren.

**1971**  Sohn Corey wird geboren.

**1972**  Fotograf bei *Sports Illustrated*.

**1978**  Verlässt *Sports Illustrated* und wechselt zu *Time*.

**1979**  Führt erstmals Regie in einem Spielfilm, *Yesterday's Hero*.

**1988**  Arbeitet während seiner Anstellung bei Time als Freier Fotograf für *Life*.

**1990**  Verlässt Time, Inc. und arbeitet zusammen mit seinem Freund, dem Chefredakteur Frank Deford, als Bildchef für *The National*.

**1991**  Leitet für *Life* während des Golfkriegs von Saudi-Arabien aus die Organisation der Foto-Berichterstattung.

**1996**  Enkel Joey wird geboren.

**1998**  Enkelin Taylor wird geboren.

**2002**  Lernt seine spätere Verlobte Randye Beth Stein kennen.

**2006**  Enkelin Riley wird geboren. Erhält den Lucie Award für bedeutende Leistungen in der Sportfotografie.

## AUSGEWÄHLTE BIBLIOGRAFIE

*Sports. A Collection of Leifer Sports Photographs.* Abrams, 1978.

*Neil Leifer's Sports Stars.* Doubleday, 1985.

*Muhammad Ali: Memories.* Rizzoli, 1992.

*Safari.* Reader's Digest, 1992.

*Sports.* Collins, 1992.

*The Best of Leifer.* Abbeville Press, 2001.

*Neil Leifer: Portraits.* St. Ann's Press, 2003.

*GOAT: A Tribute to Muhammad Ali.* TASCHEN, 2004. Einer der beiden Fotografen, die den Großteil der Aufnahmen stellten.

*A Year in Sports.* Abbeville Press, 2006.

## FILMOGRAFIE

*Yesterday's Hero,* 1979. Regisseur. Spielfilm mit Suzanne Somers und Ian McShane.

*Trading Hearts,* 1987. Regisseur. Spielfilm mit Raul Julia und Beverly D'Angelo.

*Rosebud,* 1991. Produzent, Regisseur. Kurzfilm.

*The Great White Hype,* 1992. Regisseur. Kurzfilm mit Bill Murray.

*Scout's Honor,* 1999. Produzent, Regisseur. Kurzfilm mit Alec Baldwin und Bill Murray.

*Picture Perfect,* 2001. Koproduzent. HBO-Dokumentation über die großen Sportfotografen unserer Tage.

*Smallroom Dancing,* 2002. Produzent, Regisseur. Kurzfilm.

*The Best of Leifer,* 2002. Koproduzent. Zweistündige ESPN-Dokumentation auf der Grundlage seines 2001 erschienenen Buches. Nominierung für den Emmy in der Kategorie „Herausragende Sport-Dokumentation".

*Steamed Dumplings,* 2003. Produzent, Drehbuchautor, Regisseur. Kurzfilm.

*You Write Better than You Play:* The Frank Deford Story, 2004. Produzent, Regisseur. 90-minütige ESPN-Dokumentation, die für den Emmy in der Kategorie „Herausragende Sport-Dokumentation" nominiert wird.

*God's Gift,* 2006. Produzent, Regisseur, Drehbuchautor. Kurzfilm.

*Portraits of a Lady,* 2007. Regisseur, Koproduzent. 40-minütige HBO-Dokumentation.

# NEIL LEIFER: VIE ET ŒUVRE

En 1960, les premières photos de Neil Leifer sont publiées dans *Sports Illustrated*. Il n'a que dix-sept ans. Il va bientôt réaliser plus de deux cents couvertures pour *SI*, *Time* et *People*. Il photographie quinze Jeux olympiques, quatre coupes du monde de football, dix-sept Kentucky Derbies, quinze masters de golf, un nombre incalculable de World Series, les douze premiers Superbowls et la plupart des grands combats de boxe pour le titre de champion du monde des poids lourds depuis la rencontre opposant Floyd Patterson à Ingemar Johansson en 1960. Il a également photographié toute la carrière de Muhammad Ali ! Aujourd'hui, il produit et réalise des films et, parfois, se lance dans une séance de photos.

## CHRONOLOGIE

**1942**  Betty et Abraham Leifer donnent naissance à Neil. Il grandit dans la cité Vladick en plein lower east Side à Manhattan.

**1948**  Naissance de son frère Howie.

**1952**  Devient membre du Henry Street Settlement Photo Club. Rencontre avec Johnny Iacono. Tous deux deviennent photographes sportifs et, surtout, amis.

**1956**  Livre les sandwiches de son oncle Sam, propriétaire du Stage Delicatessen dans le centre de Manhattan. Obtient souvent des pellicules en pourboire lorsqu'il livre les studios de *Life*.

**1957**  Lycéen au Seward Park high school. S'occupe des photos du journal du lycée, *The Seward World*.

**1958**  À seize ans, il aide des anciens combattants en fauteuil roulant à s'installer dans les tribunes lors de la finale NFL de football américain entre les New York Giants et les Baltimore Colts. Il y gagne une place pour le match. Prend l'une de ses photos les plus célèbres : l'essai par mort subite vainqueur d'Alan Ameche.

**1961**  Première couverture de *Sports Illustrated* : le quarterback des Giants, Y.A. Tittle.

**1965**  Prend sa photo couleur la plus connue : Muhammad Ali toise un Sonny Liston, K.-O., à terre. Épouse Renae.

**1967**  Naissance de sa fille Jodi.

**1971**  Naissance de son fils Corey.

**1972**  Devient photographe collaborateur de *Sports Illustrated*.

**1978**  Quitte *Sports Illustrated*. Devient photographe collaborateur du *Time*.

**1979**  Réalise son premier long métrage, *Yesterday's Hero*.

**1988**  Toujours collaborateur du *Time*, il devient photographe freelance pour le magazine *Life*.

**1990**  Quitte Time, Inc. pour rejoindre son ami Frank Deford, rédacteur en chef du *The National*. En devient le directeur de la photographie.

**1991**  Pendant la guerre du Golfe, chef des opérations photographiques du magazine *Life* en Arabie Saoudite.

**1996**  Naissance de son petit-fils Joey.

**1998**  Naissance de sa petite-fille Taylor.

**2002**  Rencontre sa future fiancée Randye Beth Stein.

**2006**  Naissance de sa petite-fille Riley. Reçoit le Lucie Award pour ses « réalisations sportives » dans le domaine de la photographie.

## BIBLIOGRAPHIE SELECTIONNÉE

*Sports. A Collection of Leifer Sports Photographs*. Abrams, 1978.

*Neil Leifer's Sports Stars*. Doubleday, 1985.

*Muhammad Ali : Memories*. Rizzoli, 1992.

*Safari*. Reader's Digest, 1992.

*Sports*. Collins, 1992.

*The Best of Leifer*. Abbeville Press, 2001.

*Neil Leifer: Portraits*. St. Ann's Press, 2003.

*GOAT: A Tribute to Muhammad Ali*. TASCHEN, 2004. L'un des deux principaux photographes.

*A Year in Sports*. Abbeville Press, 2006.

## FILMOGRAPHIE

*Yesterday's Hero*, 1979. Réalisateur. Long métrage avec Suzanne Somers et Ian McShane.

*Trading Hearts*, 1987. Réalisateur. Long métrage avec Raul Julia et Beverly D'Angelo.

*Rosebud*, 1991. Producteur, réalisateur. Court métrage.

*The Great White Hype*, 1992. (en version française : La couleur de l'arnaque). Réalisateur. Court métrage avec Bill Murray.

*Scout's Honor*, 1999. Producteur, réalisateur. Court métrage avec Alec Baldwin et Bill Murray.

*Picture Perfect*, 2001. Coproducteur. Documentaire de HBO sur les plus grands photographes sportifs de notre époque.

*Smallroom Dancing*, 2002. Court métrage. Producteur, réalisateur.

*The Best of Leifer*, 2002. Coproducteur et personnage principal. Documentaire de deux heures commandé par ESPN basé sur son livre de 2001. Nominé aux Emmy Awards dans la catégorie des « Documentaires sportifs exceptionnels ».

*Steamed Dumplings*, 2003. Court métrage. Producteur, auteur, réalisateur.

*You Write Better than You Play: The Frank Deford Story*, 2004. Producteur, réalisateur. Documentaire de 90 minutes commandé par la chaîne ESPN. Nominé aux Emmy Awards dans la catégorie des « Documentaires sportifs exceptionnels ».

*God's Gift*, 2006. Réalisateur, auteur, producteur. Court métrage.

*Portraits of a Lady*, 2007. Réalisateur, coproducteur. Documentaire de 40 minutes commandé par HBO.

# INDEX